The Healer's Companion

Techniques, Tips, and Tools

by Laughing Womyn Ashonosheni

Published 2021

Sophronia Press

Benton Harbor, MI 49022

~ Other works by this author ~
Radiant Wisdom Tarot
The Sacred Hoops Course
Mattie's Magical Summer
TJ Remembers The Mountain
The Wizard's Fort
The Bakery Fox
The Fool, The Empress, and The Magician
Coming Home To Me ~ Complete Healing From PTSD
Whispers of Our Knowings

Available at LaughingWomyn.com and major online retailers.

First Printing, 2021
Printed in the United States of America.

Cover design and all artwork by Laughing Womyn Ashonosheni
Photography by Suzanne Kammerer

ISBN   978-1-941301-22-7 (print)
ISBN   978-1-941301-23-4 (epub)
BISAC   OCC011000   HEA032000

Published by

Sophronia
Press

Benton Harbor, MI 49022

PRAISE FOR THE HEALER'S COMPANION

Laughing Womyn is a truly masterful healer who embodies everything she shares in this amazing treasure chest of a book!

BRET & CHRISTINE EARTHEART
Founders of the Center for Thriving Relationships

In an era when social media tells emerging healers that their validity is in the number of their followers, *The Healer's Companion* calls its readers to the heart and integrity of this sacred work. Laughing Womyn shares tried and true wisdom and healing techniques that hold healers to a grounded way of being in this world as they tend to the expansion and wholeness of humanity.

MELISSA LARIMER
LMT, Perinatal Support Provider & Spiritual Mentor

The Healer's Companion by Laughing Womyn Ashonosheni is a thorough and practical guide for those in the healing arts or for those who wish to develop the skills of healing. This book guides the reader on a journey of discovery through the many aspects of being a healer. It provides powerful tools that encourage clarity and safety for healing the self and others and takes your hand as you walk step-by-step through real-life examples.

The author's decades of personal experience and wisdom shine through as she shares her knowledge, understanding, and experience. If you are on the healing path, this book is sure to become a source of inspiration and wisdom, and it will tremendously enrich your life. I have been a professional healer for the past 20+ years and I have learned so much from what is shared in this book.

Don't pass this book by; it's well worth your time.

MATECE SKOW
ERYT-500 Founder of Nourishing Heart Yoga

INTRODUCTION

This book is an invitation and guide to expanding your skill as a healer who helps people thrive in all ways. Whether you're a healer by profession, an emerging healer, or healing is one of your personal activities, this book is a rich and practical resource for inspiration and skill development.

Every person is challenged by life and at times needs help re-balancing. Every person also needs help figuring out how to step fully into a life of win/win. Through my work with thousands of people from all over the world, I've consistently seen how very real this is and how effective healers can be at facilitating well-being that nourishes win/win.

The presence healers can bring is one of generosity, respect for self and others, and unconditional love. We know it's possible to appreciate and celebrate all forms of life and all ways of being. Carrying a commitment to fairness and equality, we embrace the wholeness and beauty of each individual. With an ever renewing hope, even in the presence of the most unsettling circumstances, healers can help bring wholeness to all we encounter.

If the idea of being a highly skilled healer inspires you, I invite you to begin where you are, engage your imagination and willingness to learn, and enjoy growing into your fullest vision of you!

Thank you for being you!

TABLE OF CONTENTS

Page

SECTION 1

THE PRESENCE OF A HEALER

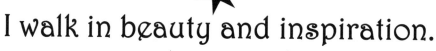

I walk in beauty and inspiration.

CHAPTER 1
DEVELOPING A WHOLENESS AFFIRMING PERSPECTIVE

Wholeness is normal and inherent in all beings.
Approaching healing from the perspective that wholeness includes everything makes space for the well-being of all without requiring the exclusion or destruction of any.

Most of us are accustomed to living through the lenses of compromise or winners and losers. This is fragmentation. When you're in situations where you tend toward compromise or win/lose, try this on instead, "All that I want and need includes each of us having all that each of us wants and needs." Wholeness makes space for everyone and everything to live the fullness of their own being.

Living the wholeness you want to help others achieve is a beautiful gift to yourself. Don't try to live every moment perfectly. Don't "try" anything. Just lovingly accept no excuses from yourself for indulging in unkindness – toward you or anyone else. When you have days or moments in which you're out of balance, wrap those experiences in unconditional love and let that love guide you into doing whatever will restore wholeness for you and everyone who was impacted by you. Trust yourself with this – your heart does know how to do it.

See everyone, including you, as right, equal, and fully empowered. See all forms of life this way - whether they're physical or spiritual. Interact with each being from the foundation that they're wise, loving, and the final authority on their own life. The process for developing this perspective is simply to consciously choose it and keep choosing it again and again until it's your natural foundation.

Every experience we have becomes a permanent part of our being. Because of this, wholeness is maintained by synthesizing and embracing every experience we have. The way to completely heal from difficult experiences is to give them permission to fulfill their purpose and become the fullness of their beauty. This allows those experiences to become part of our beauty rather than being unwelcome things we wish had never happened. A good way to do this is to love yourself absolutely and unconditionally.

Let yourself see the beauty in all imbalances and enjoy the humor in them when they show up. We often overlook the synchronicity or the goofiness of timing, location, content, or impact when we encounter or create an imbalance. When we're open to the beauty, we can see some amazing results from the imbalance.

When we're open to the humor, we can see ways to lighten the impact and maybe even relax into the situation rather than resist it.

Please remember that you know what wholeness looks like for you and you don't know what it looks like for others. You can help others discover their own wholeness. You can tell or show them what you understand it to be. You can inspire them to create it for themselves. You'll never know all the pieces that are needed for another person to live their wholeness. Only they can recognize what will bring the fullness of beauty to all levels of their being and only they can live that.

Simple Things You Can Do to Affirm Wholeness
- ♥ Listen to your body wisdom.
- ♥ Compliment people.
- ♥ Live your own definition of success. Don't try to live someone else's definition; you're not here doing the same thing they're doing.
- ♥ Encourage yourself and everyone else to think for themselves.
- ♥ Give yourself and everyone you encounter permission to be who they see themselves being.
- ♥ Smile at other people and look them in the eyes.
- ♥ Speak your truth.
- ♥ Live your truth.
- ♥ Give your heart and mind permission to lead the way together.
- ♥ Live according to your own sense of integrity.
- ♥ Choose to align with fear in ways that enhance your well-being. Fear is our biological warning about impending physical danger. It's very inaccurate when we use it to warn ourselves about potential emotional, ideological, or spiritual challenges.
- ♥ Choose to remember we're all connected – what each of us does impacts everyone else.
- ♥ Choose to do things that expand your well-being while they're expanding the well-being of everyone else.
- ♥ Choose to refrain from doing things that expand your well-being while diminishing the well-being of others. Choose to refrain from doing things that expand the well-being of others while diminishing your well-being.
- ♥ Find ways to create win-win in all situations. If even one person impacted is dissatisfied, that's one too many.
- ♥ Recognize when enough is enough. There isn't a need to have it all, be it all, keep it forever or experience it all. Choose to be consciously aware of when you've fulfilled your connection with anything, and stop there.

A Word of Encouragement

If you're new to experiencing life through the perspectives presented in this book, be patient with your growing awareness. You may find things here that take awhile to absorb and understand. A good way to work with this is to read a bit, pause for awhile and let it start settling in, then read some more. You'll understand some of the information more fully as your mind has time to play with it, some as you read further in the book, and some as you experiment with it. Trust yourself and your process with this.

CHAPTER 2
CHOOSING FULL EMPOWERMENT

The foundations of being a fully empowered person are loving yourself unconditionally and consistently showing up in ways that align with your own wisdom and integrity. When you have you, when your relationship with you is solid, kind, loving, and honest, you'll know that you can gracefully handle everything life brings your way. You'll know that, in all situations, you can trust yourself to support your own well-being and at the same time support the well-being of all others.

Part of being fully empowered is walking our own talk – being living examples of the wholeness we're encouraging others to grow into. Another part of empowerment is being living examples of how to move from being diminished by challenges into using challenges to expand our ability to be loving kindness. We don't need to do these things perfectly, or even do them well, to claim our place as healers. We just need to keep living them as well as we can while we continue expanding our ability to live them fully.

Discovering your own path into living full empowerment is made easier by being willing to understand the reasons people take actions that diminish well-being. Allowing yourself to fully understand what humans, and you personally, are trying to achieve by doing things that are contrary to well-being will help you find ways to live your own goals and visions while at the same time expanding the well-being of all who are touched by your life.

Some Ways to Expand Your Personal Power
♥ Be fully present and emotionally detached at the same time.
> This is you, being attentive, engaged, and loving while at the same time staying in your own center. One way to develop your skill with this is to intentionally put yourself in situations where other people are emotional and practice staying centered in yourself while you're there.

> If you're not yet skilled at being fully present and staying in your own center at the same time, begin practicing for short periods of time in low intensity situations. As you find yourself able to stay centered, gradually expand the time and intensity of the situations you step into.

> If you start feeling or expressing the same emotions that others are, or expressing painful or defensive emotions in response to them, you're allowing yourself to get caught up in their emotions rather than staying

centered in yourself. In situations where you're caught up in the emotions of others, take a slow, deep breath and focus on your heart. From your heart, spread love throughout your whole being. Then focus on your solar plexus and spread wisdom throughout your whole being and the entire situation. Take another slow, deep breath and then speak or act based on your own calm, clear wisdom. If you get caught up in the emotions again, repeat this.

♥ Be at ease with differences.

This is you being comfortable and confident. Many of us are the most confident and comfortable when we're in familiar situations or among people who are like us. Those are sweet places to rest. The nature of life makes it impossible to live in constant familiarity.

To develop your ease with differences, put yourself in unfamiliar situations and places and in the midst of people who are very different from you. Stay in each situation long enough to feel your difference from what you're surrounded with. If this becomes uncomfortable for you, stay just a little longer and then leave. Keep doing this until you feel at ease wherever you are.

♥ Be the safety at all times and in all situations.

This is your calm, open-hearted, confident presence. This is not defensiveness, aggression, being on guard, or displays of power or self-righteousness. Being the safety is being fully aware, fully present, and in conscious control of your own decisions and actions.

If you don't already have this skill, you can develop it by slowing down your thinking enough to catch your inner dialogue and be aware of the motivations behind your words and behavior. Good ways to do this include meditation, tai-chi and other martial arts, pausing for a minute to think before you act or speak, and making a point of interrupting your automatic responses. Do these things repeatedly until being fully aware of your motivations is a normal part of your conscious thinking.

♥ Accept no excuses from yourself.

This is you, holding you accountable to your own integrity. It's not about being rigidly prefect. It's about being honest with yourself and living with your truth rather than creating stories that excuse, justify, or explain away the times when you choose to not be all of who you really are.

♥ Use empowering language.

This is you, speaking in ways that support you and others in seeing options, making your own decisions, thinking outside the box, being confident, being kind, and living all the wonderful aspects of humanity. Information about how to develop skill with this is in Chapter 21.

♥ Be kind to yourself.

This is you, loving you. Let go of self-criticism, shaming, punishing, or demeaning. Those dynamics support what you wish you weren't. When you make a mistake, toward yourself or anyone else, take responsibility for it and do what you can to make it right.

♥ Listen to your own body wisdom.

This is you, cherishing you. Every one of us knows exactly what we need to keep all aspects of own being in optimal health and living our fullness. If you're not aware of this yet, give your body permission to tell you the truth and then pay attention to your responses to experiences, foods, sleep, activities, types of interactions, etc. When you pay attention to your body's initial responses they're typically clear, subtle, and gentle. When you consistently disregard those initial responses they tend to become more confusing, persistent, and challenging.

Uncomfortable or dissatisfied body responses indicate something that diminishes your wholeness, Pleasant or satisfied body responses indicate something that supports your wholeness. Either of these responses can be about the short term or the long term.

When your body and mind disagree with each other, here are some suggestions for resolving that dissonance and seeing your truth:

If you tend to push yourself beyond your physical, mental, or emotional comfort zone back it down a little. Move a bit slower or gentler and ease yourself into a more expanded space rather than pushing. If your body still has an adverse response, accept your body's truth and act in alignment with that.

If you tend to confine yourself to your physical, mental, or emotional comfort zone, gently coax yourself beyond that by taking one step at a time. When you get uncomfortable, pause for a bit and then take another step. If your body still has an adverse response, accept your body's truth and act in alignment with that.

♥ Work with what's real.

This is you, being honest with you. We all live with situations that we resist, don't want, or that undermine our wholeness. When you're in a situation like this, acknowledge that your own choices have taken you there. This isn't a blaming or shaming thing. This is acceptance of the fact that somewhere along the line, even if you don't know where or why, you turned toward this rather than toward something different.

Ask yourself if you're willing to continue on this course. If you are, and sometimes you truly are, choose to accept that it somehow aligns with your life purpose and you'll understand it all when the time is right. Then get pragmatic and flow with what comes with as much grace and wisdom as you're able to in each moment.

If you're not willing to continue on course, look at the options you already know about and give your mind permission to consciously find options you don't yet know about. Then take your first step in a new direction by doing the next right thing you can see. Keep taking the next right step you can see until you're satisfied with the result.

When the situation can't be changed at all or can't be changed for awhile, look for the wholeness in the bigger picture. That bigger picture may be seeing where the situation fits in the experience of your soul, where it fits in the full span of your life, or where it fits in the experience of humanity. Being able to see these bigger pictures supports our immediate wholeness by freeing creative energy we can use to change the situation or to live more of its beauty.

♥ Look through the Healing Techniques in Section 4 and work with yourself with all of them that feel right for you.

CHAPTER 3
BEING A HIGHLY SKILLED HEALER

Being a highly skilled healer comes through experience. It's a way of facilitating balance by being fully present, flowing with needs and circumstances, and using the combination of your learned skills, intuition, life experience, and openness to possibility. It's within the reach of everyone who chooses it.

Frequent use of your healing skills, combined with time, experience, observation of the results of your work, and continued learning will expand your expertise. An important part of your continued learning is focusing on growing beyond your self-imposed filters and limitations. Your work will be greatly enhanced when, in all aspects of your life, you set aside fear, beliefs about how things should be, and any desire to avoid dealing with the reality of a situation. Keeping any of these limitations or filters will make it difficult for you to accurately understand how to use the full range of healing and wholeness information you receive through touch, observation, intuition, or conversation.

Help yourself grow beyond self-imposed limitations and filters by trying on the following perspectives. If they fit for you, live them. If they're uncomfortable for you, consider exploring why.

♥ **We're equal partners with those in spirit.**
Our work as healers is an equal partnership with Spirit. Those on the spirit plane do the things that are best done with their type of energy and skills, we do what's best done with ours. Experiencing the differences and the partnership of those two planes is part of our purpose for experiencing life and death.

In our "separation" from each other, there's no hierarchy. No one has power over another, and no one is of service to the will of another. There's simply a meeting of hearts, souls, and skills that's capable of manifesting things that seem to be impossible.

My experience with this:
For a long time, I believed in a spiritual hierarchy. I'd grown up with that belief and just didn't question it. When I was introduced to the idea that we're equal partners with those in Spirit, I felt my mind opening, reaching for something I'd always known yet couldn't quite touch. As I played with the implications of the idea, I'd embrace it for a little while, then push it away again. Then, in my body and my mind, it started making sense. It was

like long lost memories returned and I gradually recognized something so familiar that I couldn't believe I hadn't recognized it before.

♥ **We choose to be here.**

Of our own free will, we choose our time on the physical plane and on the spiritual plane. We also choose our families and many of the challenges we'll encounter during a specific lifetime. The glimpses I have about why we do this indicate that we're curious, growing, evolving beings who like to immerse ourselves in a large variety of experiences. We do this to help ourselves learn how to keep our hearts wide open in the midst of every possible reality.

My experience with this:

I really resisted embracing this one. For years, I felt like I'd lost a poker game and ended up in this lifetime as some sort of bad joke. That perspective crumbled for me after I'd lived enough years to look back along the meandering trail I took while seeking a life that I could enjoy. From the perspective of those years, I could see how the many different ways I'd earned a living provided me with the skills I needed to be self-employed and doing work I love. I could see how my own confusion and intense emotional challenges had inspired me to learn many of the skills I use as a healer. It's not that I couldn't have learned these things in gentler ways. It's just that, until I'd lived what I lived, I had no idea where I was trying to go or the gentler ways to get there.

♥ **As a healer you're limitless.**

You can be a healer in all situations, throughout time and space, across species and geography, whether the ones you're working with are embodied or in spirit, in this universe or any other. You can simultaneously participate in helping to heal multiple imbalances in multiple locations, beings, and times. You can do all of this in ways that enhance your well-being while you're helping others enhance their own well-being.

My experience with this:

One way I use this perspective is by keeping an open mind during each client session. In addition to the foundational approaches I use, I stay alert to what I observe and hear in my interactions with the person I'm working with and to any intuitive messages I'm receiving. Then I move with my inspiration about how to combine those things to support the growth or healing my client is seeking.

Another way is by working in the dreamtime. Many years ago I made an agreement with Spirit that I'm happy to do healing work during my dreamtime for anyone anywhere as long as it enhances my sleep. To do this, I just sleep. If I wake up in the midst of a dream that includes me helping someone else, instead of trying to figure it out, I just take a second to enjoy the fact that I can work this way and then I go back to sleep. Being available this way has turned out to be one of the gifts I love about being a healer.

I also do this in everyday situations by assuming that if I notice a situation and it bothers me in any way, it means I can do something about it. In these situations, my first step is to consider what I can easily do to help restore balance. If I feel blocked for any reason from doing something helpful on the physical plane, I pause for a second, open my heart, and send wholeness to all involved. I stay with this until I feel my energy stop flowing into the situation. Then I let it go and I move on.

♥ **Side effects indicate imbalance.**
Side effects are the result of using incomplete or ineffective approaches to healing. Damaging something to make something else healthier is a compromise that doesn't create health or wholeness - it shifts damage from one form to another. Facilitate wholeness rather than accepting side effects.

♥ **Fear's only purpose is to alert us to imminent physical danger.**
Through family and cultural perspectives and belief systems, we've become accustomed to experiencing fear in response to situations that are unrelated to imminent physical danger. This is exhausting to our adrenal system and reduces our ability to respond effectively to potential accidents, violence, and other physical health challenges. Please consider re-balancing this in yourself by remembering that you're the only one who can choose how you respond to your life experiences.

Learn from Yourself

Whether you're working with a client, receiving healing yourself, or participating in a daily activity, approaching every experience as a learning opportunity will support your awareness of what's really possible, what causes imbalance, what supports balance, and what inspires growth. Keep your heart and mind open to the insights you receive just through living each day.

My experience with this:
In my early years as a healer, I had many opportunities to notice that the distance from my mouth to my clients' ears is usually much shorter than the distance

from my mouth to my own ears. During sessions, I often caught myself sharing insights and wisdoms that I didn't apply to my own life. In noticing that, I discovered that one of the best ways to expand my skill as a healer, and my own wholeness, is to listen to the wisdoms I give to others and put them into action in my own life.

Be a Sacred Witness to Your Own Process

This is our deepest, most permanent way of expanding our healing skills. Lived experience synthesizes into all levels of our beings in ways that theories and observations just don't. Regardless of who we are or how we live, each of us have experiences that we use to create imbalance in ourselves. Notice how I said that – experiences that we use… This is a truth we often fail to notice when we don't look at ourselves deeply and compassionately.

When we allow ourselves to be a neutral, loving witness to our own process we can easily see our imbalances and how we justify them, our blind spots and how we maintain them, our beauty and how we share that, and our motivations for doing all of those things. We can also easily see how to create balance in ourselves and engage our natural compassion and integrity in response to ourselves and others.

My Experience With This:
Being a sacred witness to myself has shown me that healing and growth can be very easy and quick. In this role, I have no reason to hide anything from myself; I have no need to deny or resist my own truths. I just notice them and consciously choose whether to continue on course or do something different. I see my wounds, ignorance, willingness to be unkind or short-sighted, generosity, love, kindness, wisdom, internal stories, justifications, and all the rest of me.

Within the spectrum of my responses to life, I also see my own paths to being a kinder, wiser me. And my paths are easy for me to walk. Because they're native to me, they don't require the learning and maintenance that's needed to successfully walk someone else's path. This way of expanding my wholeness continues to be quite an education about humanity and the things that actually motivate us to live the best of who we are.

Notice and Use What's Naturally in Your Environment

We can't always control the environment we're working in. Instead of allowing that to disturb our work, we can embrace it as part of the work. This is the core of being able to facilitate healing wherever you are at the time it's needed.

Make a point of thinking creatively, being intuitively open, and being observant of your environment. What you notice may be plants, stones, a nearby stream, the call or presence of animals… It may be the 90-degree angle of a corner, the color of a sweater, the air temperature, mechanical noises… Assume that what catches your attention can somehow help facilitate wholeness; then pause for a second and invite those things to help.

Give yourself permission to be a healer who knows how to work with the richness of all that is around you in addition to using your learned skills and familiar supplies.

My Experience With This:
One of the best pieces of advice I received as a young healer was to fold everything that happens into the power of the session. If a loud truck goes by and disrupts the tranquility of the moment, remind my client that everything is flowing together to support their wholeness. If the client falls asleep during a guided meditation, same thing… Knowing how to do this allows me to do my work in all types of environments, including noisy, unpredictable, public spaces.

Find the Possible in the Impossible
Impossible is what we call things we don't yet know how to do. Believing that impossible is a permanent condition is contrary to the observable evidence all around us. Everything here on Earth is in a constant process of change and embracing this reality helps us remember there's still a lot for us to discover. Give yourself permission to know that impossible means the path to what lies beyond impossible has yet to be seen.

My Experience With This
When I think I've reached the end of what's possible, and I'm not satisfied with that end, I turn to the combination of my questions, intuition, and willingness to persist. I reach into the illogical, the what if, and the don't-even-consider-it. Sometimes that feels very ungrounded and chaotic. I've done this enough to know those feelings are present because I'm sorting through possibilities so quickly that my conscious mind can't keep up. I let that be what it is and keep sorting until I feel the presence of something that has substance. Regardless of how logical or illogical that possibility appears to be, I work with it and see where it goes.

Choose Practicality
Regardless of all the insights and options we can provide through various aspects of our work, our clients need tangible results and that requires practicality on

our part. Help your clients enjoy the sustainable results of their work with you by teaching them easy ways to integrate and support their own wholeness. Help them see how your insights can be applied to the life they currently live. Doing simple things like offering several ideas and asking your client to choose one that sounds easy to them, can help them understand how to build on the work you've done together.

Here are some ideas:

- ♥ Provide information about how to be gentle during the next 24 – 48 hours while their body integrates the healing session.
- ♥ Together, create an action plan for living their intentions.
- ♥ Offer examples of ways to integrate wholeness into their daily lives.
- ♥ Provide "homework" they can do on their own.

Embrace Dichotomy

"Both and" is a perspective that makes space for inclusion. It embraces the reality that very different understandings of the same experiences, information, and ideas can all be equally true and valid. Choosing to enjoy dichotomy helps us remember how to flow gracefully with all that life brings and how to help our clients do the same.

To expand your capacity for embracing "both and", play with a variety of ideas that appear to be contradictory or mutually exclusive. Keep playing until you see how they can all be true and valid and can work together. A good one to begin with is the dichotomy of "both and" and "either or"; one includes all; the other excludes some.

Be Fully Present

Give yourself permission to be fully there for each moment of your life. Developing this skill isn't about perfection on your part. It's about noticing when you forget to do this, gently guiding yourself back to it, and trusting yourself to expand this skill every time you use it.

Discover Healing & Wholeness Techniques

The question of how to heal anything is simply this, "How can I support this in becoming the fullness of its being?" From that question, let your creative thinking flow into possibilities. Try on the first thought that comes to your mind in response to that question. Don't over think it, just try it on.

- ♥ If it's something that could bring harm or diminish well-being, set it aside and move on to the next idea that comes to your mind.

- ♥ If it's something that doesn't diminish well-being and won't bring any harm, work with it in some way and see if an effective approach emerges from it.
- ♥ If no thought comes to you, take a gentle breath, give your conscious mind permission to receive an answer, and know that the answer will come when the moment is right.

When you're working this way during a session, check in with your client as you work. Ask if they feel comfortable or aligned with what you're doing. Watch their body language for signs of comfort, discomfort, openness, guardedness, etc. If your client is uncomfortable in any way, gently adjust what you're doing until they're comfortable. Then continue with whatever makes sense next. "Pain no gain" is a good guide when you're working this way – if you or your client are uncomfortable in any way, something you're doing needs to be shifted.

My Experience With This:
When I started allowing myself to be creative this way I had no proof that any of the ideas I came up with had any substance to them. Although each one felt right in the moment, I felt like I was dreaming things up and I wasn't confident about their effectiveness. Through the course of the next several years, I received plenty of feedback that this part of my work was effective and I began relaxing into it more.

Now, when I find myself working with a situation I don't understand, I'm confident about my ability to intuitively find an effective way to help my client. While I'm listening to my client, I'm also thinking and searching, opening my mind to what could help. This feels to me like I'm rapidly flipping through a library catalog, watching out of the corner of my eye for a hint of an answer. When that hint appears, it feels like a fit even though I usually catch only a whisper of it. Holding that whisper of a path toward wholeness, I start guiding my client to it. As I speak each word, more words come to my mind and I keep going until the path is obvious and the work is flowing.

This has become part of what intrigues me about being a healer. I'm fascinated with the endless variety of healing and growth techniques that fit one single moment and then disappear, and the endless variety that become an ongoing part of my work.

CHAPTER 4
ETHICS OF BEING A HEALER

This is an overview of the general ethics most healers voluntarily work within. If any of your modalities require government licensing, or have a professional association, you may be required to work within other ethical practices.

♥ Before touching or advising anyone, ask for their permission.

♥ Suspend your own agendas, perspectives, and judgments and be open to your client's truth.

♥ Work from the intention of supporting the highest good of everyone involved.

♥ Maintain confidentiality. Unless a client has given you permission to talk with others about them or their experience with you, who you work with and what occurs during sessions is confidential. Even if a session appears to be light-hearted or about unimportant topics, what occurred belongs to your client. What they share about their work with you is up to them.

♥ Talking about your work is important sometimes. When that's the case, talk in ways that can't reveal, or hint at, the identity of any of your clients. Talk about the type of work you do, the value of it, the impact it has on you, your experience of facilitating that type of session, and questions that come up for you about your work.

♥ If you receive insights or messages for a client during a session, give her/him all of the message that you feel is both accurate and complete. Provide the information clearly and in practical terms so your client knows how to apply it to their life. Messages you receive for or about clients belong to them. It's not your responsibility to decide what your client can handle knowing. If your client doesn't connect with the message, tell them it's ok, you may have gotten the message wrong or they may connect with it later. Your responsibility is to give the message in a clear, loving, supportive way and if desired by your client, help her/him embrace it.

♥ When a session reveals current or potential challenges, provide your client with information about how to prevent those challenges or how to live them gracefully.

♥ Sometimes we're called on to work without permission from the people or beings we're trying to help. In those situations, send energy for the greatest good of all who are impacted by the situation and don't define the energy any more specifically than that. Remember – the outcome you think should occur may not be for the greatest good. Leave defining the outcome to the souls of all who are impacted by it.

Respecting Free Will

Healing is most effective when it's facilitated and received with full respect for the free will of everyone impacted by it.

For healers, this means facilitating sessions with no desire to influence the client and with no attachment to how or if the client follows through on any information given during the session. A perspective that supports this is, "You and I have engaged in this time of healing and learning. How or if you use it is for you to decide."

Clients sometimes request information for or about people who aren't present during the session. The ethics of answering this type of question can be delicate. It can be appropriate when your client has responsibility for the other person's well-being; it's usually inappropriate when that isn't the situation. If you have any hesitation about answering this type of question, just don't do it. It's perfectly ok to not provide insights for or about people who aren't present at the session.

SECTION 2

WORKING AS A HEALER

Love is present here.

CHAPTER 5
HOLDING SPACE FOR HEALING

Creating Healing Space

Wherever and however you do your work, you're the still-point that shifts the energy into a healing space. Move gently and kindly. Speak clearly, evenly, and calmly. Touch in ways that soothe and relax. Allow yourself to be the point of reference for the person you're working with.

Be fully present to the person's process and if they get distracted, call their attention back to you and the moment. This can be done very gently by asking them to pause or to look into your eyes for a second and breathe with you.

When outside noises or movements impact the person you're working with, gently remind them to breathe, relax into the outside influence, and know it's happening right then because it supports their healing process.

If you're working by phone or online video, your attentiveness, tone of voice, and a reliable connection are essential. Dropped or weak cell signals, unreliable internet connections, and other technical problems disrupt your ability to provide guidance to your client. For phone sessions, I find that using a land line on my end is the most reliable way to support clear conversations.

Setting the Atmosphere

Confidentiality is the foundation of creating a space where people feel free to share and experience all they need to. What occurs between you and your client is never yours to share. If your client chooses to share their experience, that's up to them. If you're working in a group, let everyone know it's ok to share their own experience outside of the group, and it's not ok to talk about what anyone else said or did.

Align your ways of interacting with your core intentions as a healer and with your intentions in each session. This includes your timing in speaking, tone of voice, and the words you choose. It includes your ways of touching, moving, standing, and sitting during the session. It includes your ways of welcoming people into your space and saying goodbye when the session ends.

When you're working with people who are experiencing emotional challenges, be calm, honest, and gently encouraging. Be a sacred witness who knows there's nothing wrong with them, their response, or the fact that they experienced what they did. Come from the perspective that they're in the process of integrating challenging experiences that are transforming into aspects of their beauty.

Holding Space Without Controlling the Space

It's important for you to set a tone of empowerment and respect for the people you work with. When someone comes to you for a session, they've given their permission for you to help them heal and grow. They haven't given permission to feel controlled by you during the session. Particularly with people who are new to you, ask permission before touching and gently communicate what will happen next by using words or touch.

If the type of work you're doing is best facilitated by you giving instructions, say something like this: I'd like you to… or please… keep your eyes closed through this… stay with yourself rather than speaking… tell me when that feels complete… sit up…, etc.

Stay completely focused on your client and their process. Notice the things that aren't being said, notice what they're saying with their words and actions, notice the energies moving through their body and aura. Tend to these things as much as you tend to the things your client is sharing in more obvious ways.

If you're working in a group, don't allow people to interrupt each other's processes. If someone does interrupt, gently remind them to hold their own energy until the current process is complete. This can be done with gentle words, a gentle touch, a finger held to your lips while you smile and look kindly at the one who's interrupting…

CHAPTER 6
SHAPING YOUR SESSIONS

Session Foundations to Consider

- ♥ The person came to receive what you have to offer.
- ♥ Receiving unconditional love and acceptance from you is part of your clients' healing.
- ♥ Fully accept the wisdom of your client's life and current process.
- ♥ Meet the person where they are mentally, emotionally, and spiritually and from there, help them find new options.
- ♥ Provide for the person's physical comfort when possible.
- ♥ Be fully present and honest.
- ♥ Let humor or playfulness flow naturally during the session.
- ♥ Support your clients' personal empowerment.
- ♥ Teach holistic skills as you move through each session.
- ♥ Provide your clients with clear, practical information about possibilities they can create and ways to bring those possibilities into their lived reality.
- ♥ Let go of the person at the end of the session.

Making the Flow of a Session Fit You

Being comfortable in the framework of your sessions will deepen the quality of the session for your client and make your work more enjoyable for you.

Length of time

Most healers offer sessions that are anywhere from 15 minutes to 2 hours long. Some offer longer sessions, even as long as several days. Offer the length(s) of time that works best for you. The key is that you offer enough time to do the work your clients come to you for and you don't make the session so long that you get tired, bored, or impatient.

Some healers work on clock time, allowing sessions to be a scheduled length of time. Others work on completion time, allowing sessions to be as brief or lengthy as needed.

One way to discern your best length of time is to observe how long you stay gently focused and fully present in ordinary activities. Another way is to let your body be a pendulum to reveal your right length of time.

Here's a process for doing that:

1. Sit in a relaxed position with your eyes closed and focus your attention on your solar-plexus.
2. Ask your body to show you a "yes" and notice how your body responds.

3. Ask your body to show you a "no" and notice how your body responds.

4. Take a slow, deep breath and ask your body to show you the right length of sessions for you.

5. Begin by saying, "5 minutes" and then pause and notice how your body responds. Then keep going with different lengths of time, varying between shorter and longer (10 minutes, 4 hours, 1 hour, 30 minutes…) until you get a definite "yes" from your body. "Maybe" isn't what you're looking for here – it will give you a session length that maybe works for you.

6. When you get that definite "yes", you've found the session length that will work for you on all levels.

My Experience With This:

I've tried both clock time and completion time and have found that I prefer completion time. If a client's needs can be addressed in five or ten minutes, I congratulate both of us on being very efficient and adjust my fee accordingly. If it looks likely that we'll go beyond the scheduled amount of time, I let the client know about 10 minutes before our scheduled end time and tell them how much longer I can continue and that the session fee will increase to match that. If they want to continue we do. If they want to complete on time, we do.

Content

Your niche as a healer is yours alone so don't try to be everything to everyone. You may be uncomfortable working with some types of challenges or ways of growing and you may not have the skill set to work with others. It's ok. Work with what you're passionate about, interested in, skilled with, and/or what brings joy to you when a client has their breakthrough.

Types of interactions

Sessions can include a wide variety of interactions between you and your clients. Make sure you're completely comfortable with every type of interaction you include. Touch, singing/chanting, conversation, movement, prayer, contact with those in spirit, emotional expressions, etc. may all come up depending on how you conduct sessions. If you're uncomfortable with any of those things, design your sessions to avoid them.

Moving Through a Session

Starting a session

It's easiest to quickly get in the flow of a session if you begin all of your sessions in pretty much the same way. The basics to include are:

- ♥ Center yourself before your client arrives and be prepared to stay fully present to them, without interruption, until the session is complete.
- ♥ Set the tone of the session in the way you greet your client.
- ♥ Give your client any additional instructions they need to be fully present for the session.
- ♥ After your client has settled in, ask what's on their mind or what's going on that brought them to you. Sometimes it's beneficial to repeat what you heard them say so you know you fully understand.
- ♥ Meet your client where they are. Trying to shift their perspective at the beginning of the session generally isn't productive. Meeting them in the perspective they're familiar with helps your client know you support their well-being. With that in place, you can gently show them how to step into other possibilities.

From there on, the modality you're working with will determine where you go.

Discerning the root of a challenge
The root cause of an imbalance is always discernable and, for me, it's the most efficient point at which to begin healing.

Discerning the root is a process of listening to your client's explanation or story while feeling for the place where everything feels aligned with truth.

People come into sessions with varied clarity about what's causing an imbalance. Some can articulate the root of an issue very clearly and succinctly. Some demonstrate it with their body rather than using words. Some share long stories that include the root, even though they're unable to identify which part of the story that is. Some are focused so deeply on the results of the root imbalance that they can't yet see the difference between the root and the results. And some roots may be things the person has no language to explain.

Common types of roots:
In the indications of these roots I mention "A feeling…" several times. That feeling may come to you while you're working with a client or it may be a feeling your client has.
- ♥ Current lifetime trauma, disability, belief system, etc.

    People can often articulate current life experiences that cause their deep challenges, though they may not always connect the initial experience with some of the challenges that have grown from it. When a client has already done significant work with a current life experience, and still doesn't feel balanced, the true root may be one of the other roots on this list. Sometimes, a current life experience is the thing we use to guide ourselves to the deeper root.

Some indications of a current lifetime root:

- Your client already knows the initial experience and the challenge are connected to each other.
- You see or feel the direct connection between the initial experience and the challenge.

♥ Soul Agenda

Before coming into a lifetime, we choose the things we want to make sure we do during that lifetime. This includes life purpose, our own growth, and things we want to contribute to life on Earth. The details of how and when we do these things are shaped by our life circumstances and experiences.

Some indications of a soul agenda root:

- Your client repeatedly engages in, or focuses on the same dynamic without knowing why.
- A belief or feeling that a clear path will be available after a specific thing happens.

♥ Past-life experience

People who know how to access their own past-life memories can often identify these roots and talk about them. People who haven't yet accessed these past-life memories will feel the truth of what you say when you've identified the true root. Sometimes it just makes sense to them. Sometimes they'll quickly recall current life experiences that somehow reflect the past-life events you tell them about.

Some indications of a past-life root:

- A feeling of something coming toward you from far away – like an echo of vision, sound, or sensation
- A feeling that your attention is being drawn to the past, to one side, or behind your body

♥ Future-life intentions

Most of us live in a steady flow of creating our future and that includes future lifetimes. When we try to live a future-life intention during our current lifetime, the challenges we create can appear to be insurmountable.

Some indications of a future-life root:

- A feeling that the challenge isn't anchored to a foundation.
- A feeling that your attention is being drawn forward or being drawn toward something that lacks substance.

♥ Soul Contracts/Soul Agreements

These are agreements we make with other souls between lifetimes, or sometimes at the end of a lifetime. We make these agreements to ensure that one or both of us stay on track about something we intend to do during an upcoming lifetime. When either soul completes their part of the agreement, their side of the contract is completed regardless of what the other soul does.

One way soul contracts show up is through the people involved feeling an irresistible draw to one another and a sense of big importance in their connection. The length of the connection is irrelevant to this, though because of the intensity, it's often seen as something that's meant to last a long time. Another way soul contracts show up is through a brief, unexpected encounter that has a profound impact on one or both people. Some indications of a soul contract root:
- A feeling that something is about to complete or has just completed.
- A point of upcoming closure that's obvious in your client's energy.

♥ Karmic connections

Some people are very aware of karmic connections, others have a vague feeling that something is going on that's unexplainable and beyond their control. When someone completes their part of the karma, they're finished with it regardless of what's done by others involved in the karmic connection.

Some indications of a karmic root:
- A feeling that a longstanding imbalance is coming into balance or that an old agenda has been fulfilled.
- A feeling of wide-open, expansive space in the near future.

My Experience With This:

When I feel like a puzzle piece fell perfectly into place I know we've reached the root or are very near to it. I pause for a second and double check that within myself. If the feeling holds, I shift the conversation by saying something like, "Let's pause right here for a minute." Then I share what came together for me and I ask my client if this resonates or feels true to them. If it does, I shift to whatever healing process is appropriate. If what I shared doesn't resonate with the person, we continue our conversation until I feel another puzzle piece fall into place. I continue this process of listening then giving insight until the person I'm working with feels the resonance of their own truth.

In these situations, "what comes together for me" is usually a combination of what the client said and something that falls into place in my own mind … a message from the spirit side, an insight from the person's energy, a wisdom or insight I hold from previous experiences, or any other combination of subtle information I received.

Moving toward wholeness

Continue being fully present to and accepting of what your client says and doesn't say and what you perceive. The combination of their wisdom and yours will guide both of you into the fullness of the session.

Here are some basics for doing this:
- ♥ Be open to all possibilities by setting aside your perspectives about your client and the issues they're working with.
- ♥ Listen deeply and fully to your client's words and watch their body language.
- ♥ Notice things that strike you as odd or out of place... missing words, unfinished thoughts, convoluted ideas, contradictory statements or body language, changes in tone of voice or volume, defensive or demeaning words or actions... When any of these things show up, your client is showing you a path to the next step in their healing process.
- ♥ Notice your client's body energy and aura. Flashes of blue or white light and brightening or intensifying aura colors indicate places where energy is moving toward wholeness. Murky or muddy aura colors indicate places where confusion is expanding or solidifying. A transparent human shape showing partially outside of one side of your client's body indicates a desire to avoid a truth they carry. When you notice these things, gently touching your client in those areas, or asking your client to gently touch those areas, will help their energy move into wholeness.
- ♥ Keep observing, feeling, and listening for a point where you feel the pieces coming together. When you feel that, pause and let your client know what you've observed and what you think it may mean.
- ♥ After sharing your observations or insights, make space for your client's truth by asking her/him if what you said feels true to them.
- ♥ If your observations or insights don't feel true to your client, you've either interpreted through your own filters or it's not the right time for your client to integrate what you've shared. Either way, let your client's truth be what it is and move on with the session in a constructive way.

My Experience With This

During sessions I often notice something unusual in my client's body language, movement, how something is said, or what's not said. When that occurs, I listen to Spirit with one ear while continuing to flow with our current interaction. I'm listening both for intuitive information from Spirit and for the person I'm working with to say something that adds to what I noticed. If the additional information gives me the sense there's more to do, I begin working with the person about whatever it is.

Working with the synergy between you and your client

At some point in each session, you'll feel the connection and flow between you and your client. You'll be in step with one another in a way that moves easily and you'll be trading leadership back and forth. This is the point where the two of you are relating energetically and your work can surpass what either of you are consciously aware is happening.

Sometimes this can be a confusing time in the session, a time when you're not sure what's yours, what's your client's, or what's coming from Spirit. If you feel confusion at all, take a deep slow breath, ground yourself, and silently affirm that all is in keeping with the greatest good of all involved.

When you're feeling grounded in the synergy, follow what comes up and move with it in ways that are respectful of your client's free will. A session is a dynamic interaction. You or your client may say or do something that draws the session into an unexpected direction. Going with the flow of that can lead the session right to the place your client didn't know they really need to be.

My Experience With This:
When synergy comes alive, I'm consciously aware that I'm quickly receiving information with all my senses including intuition. I'm present to the person I'm with and the environment around us and I'm gathering insight from all of it. Even though I don't have time to consciously sort through each insight I receive, I'm consciously aware that it's all blending into something understandable.

While this process continues in the background of my mind, I keep interacting with my client, sometimes giving them insight about something we've already explored, sometimes following their lead into something new. When the whole process is completed, information stops flowing in and there's suddenly nothing more to say or do about whatever it was. That completes that focus for the session, but it may not be the end of the session. This kind of flow can occur many different times during a session, each with a different focus and each lasting anywhere from a couple of minutes to an hour or longer.

Using multiple modalities in one session

Most healers who know more than one form of healing use a variety of modalities in each session. As long as you're comfortable with the shift and you integrate it into the session flow, your clients will shift with you very easily.

Knowing when to shift:

♥ Follow your intuition – when you feel what comes next, it's time to shift.
♥ Follow your client – when they get restless or resist what you're doing, it's time to shift.
♥ Follow your body – when your body wants to move on, it's time to shift.
♥ Follow your thoughts – when they start to stray, it's time to shift.

Some gentle approaches to these transitions:

♥ From one form of hands-on-healing to another – keep one hand in place for a few seconds while you begin the new technique with the other hand.
♥ From hands-on-healing to hands-off or talking – continue to touch your client for a few seconds while you begin the next process.
♥ From talking to another form of healing or teaching – say something like, "Let's shift course a little here…"
♥ From one form of hands-off energy work to another – imagine the shift happening in a gentle flow of energy from one place to another.

Staying present to your client

Through the course of a session there are often quiet moments when the energy feels like it's paused or you're waiting for the next aspect to be revealed. There may be moments when your client repeats something you've addressed before and your ability to be present to their need to repeat is a bit low. There may be moments when your client presents something you're uncomfortable with, don't want to respond to, or don't know how to respond to.

These spaces between you and your client are great times to let your client be with their own process and their own truth. For a few seconds or minutes, stay present to your client without interacting. You can use these times to integrate or ground yourself a bit by distancing your energy just enough to also be more present to yourself for a minute or so.

When you feel the energy shift a little, check in with your client by saying something to the effect of "Tell me what's present for you right now" or "Tell me how you're feeling right now." Then continue with the session.

Ending a session

If you work on clock time, give your client time to reach completion by starting to guide the session to closure about ten minutes before you want to be done.

If you work on completion time, notice when the energy begins slowing down or dropping off. This often feels like quiet or stillness returning to your healing space. When you feel this, ask your client if they're feeling complete and if they are, begin bringing the session to closure.

It's important for your clients to be fully present to their ordinary life when they leave a session. They need to be able to get home safely and to continue integrating the healing when they're in their normal environment. Gentle, clear completion of each session will support this. A simple way to end a session is to ask your client if they feel complete and fully present. If they don't, take another few minutes to help settle their energy in some way. If they do feel complete, guide them through a simple series of grounding activities… a drink of cool water, stretching, paying for the session, sharing a hug with you…

When a client lingers, and you don't want them to, here are some suggestions:
- ♥ If you have time to extend the session, let your client know the session fee will increase and then work with them a bit longer if they want that.
- ♥ Offer to schedule another session.
- ♥ Let them know another client is scheduled soon, or that you have to get on to something else.
- ♥ Walk them out of your space, and maybe all the way to their car. Then give a hug and walk away.
- ♥ Suggest they sit outside or take a short walk until they feel grounded.
- ♥ With clients who consistently linger, tell them what your fees are for longer sessions and offer to schedule one for them.

Letting go at the end of the session
Providing a healing session is a very specific way of relating and it lives only for the time of the session. When that time is complete, give your client space to fully hold their own experience by stopping your flow of energy toward them until they come to you for another session.

To support yourself in this, center and ground yourself after your client leaves and before you begin another session or engage in other activities. Some ways to do this:
- ♥ Drink a glass of water.
- ♥ Eat a root food - this is any food with an edible part that grows underground.
- ♥ Go outside and touch the ground with your bare hands or feet.
- ♥ Smudge yourself and your healing space.
- ♥ Do a few minutes of vigorous physical movement, stretching, or dance.
- ♥ Hold a grounding stone in your hand for a few minutes. Some good stones for grounding are: ordinary pebbles or gravel, hematite, black tourmaline.
- ♥ Sing, chant, or drum.

Relating to Clients During Sessions

A large part of a healer's work is teaching people how to create and sustain their own wholeness. While you're working with clients, also teach them how to know and trust their own body, energy, and wisdom. Teach them how to love themselves. Help them understand why they go out of balance and options they have for preventing that. Teach them how to notice when they're out of balance and simple ways they can restore balance. Most of all, help them learn to love and live all of who they are.

Being a sacred witness to your client's process

Part of our role as healers is to be present for clients in ways that accept them as normal, capable, fully empowered people. Regardless of someone's choices, imbalances, challenges, limitations, or lack of information, when we respond in relaxed open-hearted ways they get to experience themselves as a welcome part of humanity. This is being a sacred witness. Unfortunately, being fully accepted by another person is a rare occurrence for many people. Sometimes being fully accepted is the only healing that's needed.

Gentle encouragement

Some people are timid or insecure during a session. Remember that your type of work may be completely new to them. They may not know what to expect of themselves; what you expect of them; or what you're going to do. They may be uncomfortable about their emotions or the reasons they're seeing you. When people haven't had permission to just be who they are in every moment of their life; they approach interactions as though they have to look, act, or respond a certain way.

Give them permission to just be who they are by gently encouraging them to relax. Assure them that their emotions are welcome and the only right way to move through the session is the way they do it. If they forget that during the session, remind them with a gentle statement such as, "You're doing this very well. Your body knows exactly how to do this; just be with whatever is present for you right now."

Listening between the words

When you're listening to a client, watching and listening for the following can reveal points of blockage or direct paths to forward movement or resolution:

♥ Contradictions, rationalizations, or places where the connection between thoughts is missing. Any of these dynamics can indicate aspects of the situation your client finds confusing, uncomfortable, unsettling, or they want to experience one way and are actually experiencing a different way.

When this type of dynamic shows up, it can be helpful to ask your client how one perspective or thought connects to the other.

♥ What your client isn't saying – among other things this can include unasked questions that are obvious to you, emotions they show without talking about them, avoidance of saying a specific word or name, etc. Any of these can indicate lack of information or avoidance. When this type of dynamic shows up, it can be helpful for you to say what your client isn't saying and ask if what you said makes sense to them, resonates with them, or is what they were trying to say.

♥ What your client is saying – this includes:
  - Speaking from victim perspective…
    (he did… to me, I couldn't stop myself…, etc.).
    When victim perspective shows up, it can be helpful to ask your client to own their power by focusing on their own response to the experience.
  - Defending
    (If… hadn't happened I would have…, I did that because…, etc.).
    When defensiveness shows up, it can be helpful to ask your client to reword their statement by saying something to this effect, "I chose to respond to that by…."
  - Detaching from self by using second or third person pronouns to speak about something they did or didn't do
    (everyone feels that way, when…happens it makes you…, when… happens you…, etc.).
    When detachment shows up, it can be helpful to ask your client to own the experience by using "I".

♥ Body language – when your client's body is relaxed and they're looking directly at you, they're comfortable being present to whatever you're focusing on. When your client's body is tightened or closed in some way (arms crossed, feet bouncing, avoiding eye contact, etc.) it can be helpful to touch them gently; ask them to take a slow deep breath and look at you; or ask them to relax the areas of their body where you're noticing stress.

Pain stories

When people seek healing, it's usually because something in their life is challenging them in ways they don't know how to handle effectively. In this place, people often live within what I call "pain stories". The person's pain story is their way of explaining what's out of balance and it's normal for these stories to be shared during a session. When listening to someone's pain story, please remember that you can help your client heal their response to the challenge and integrate the experience in ways that add to their beauty, but you can't erase the fact that the challenge occurred.

If your client's emotional intensity increases while they're sharing a pain story, or if they start repeating things they've already said, gently ask your client to pause and take a deep breath. When you feel their energy calm or clarify a bit, ask them to continue.

My Experience With This:
The way I do this is to say something like, "please pause here and take a deep gentle breath." I stay in my own physical space and take a deep breath myself, giving my client a physical example of what to do. Then I sit silently for a few seconds and let my client feel the stillness.

When the time feels right, I say something like, "please tell me what's present for you right now." This is a request for the client to verbalize the emotions, thoughts, or physical sensations they're experiencing right in that moment. It gives another little space of time for them to disengage from the thought loop or intense emotions they were in. After that I ask them a question to restart the conversation we had paused.

This simple process reminds people that it's possible to relate to the disturbance calmly. It gives them a physical experience of calming their own emotions and returning to their center, even when they're in the thick of an emotional escalation.

Finding the core of the pain story
While you're listening to a pain story, listen for the core of the whole dynamic rather than responding to the details or the emotions about it. The core is the entry door for healing. When you think you've heard the core, listen another minute or so, holding the core in mind, until you feel a sense of confirmation that you've found it. Then gently pause the conversation for a few seconds before guiding your client into a healing process.

My Experience With This:
The way I do this is to listen quietly until something stands out. Then I listen just a little longer to make sure what stood out is the entry door for healing. When I've found this, it feels to me like a puzzle piece just slipped into place and my mind stops searching. I often find myself thinking something like, "ah, there it is."

At that point I gently say something like, "Let's pause right here. I just heard what I need to know." Then, without explaining what I heard, I begin my work.

Working with a healing crisis

A healing crisis is a client's intensely uncomfortable response to their own growth or healing. This occurs when the client's energy and aura re-balance so quickly that the slower moving physical aspects of their mind, body, or emotions feel misaligned. Most people don't experience this. When someone does, it can look pretty dramatic while it's in process.

Usually a healing crisis occurs suddenly during, or shortly after, a session and can be fully re-balanced within a matter of minutes or days. The way your client experiences this can be any combination of physical, mental, emotional, or spiritual confusion, fear, discomfort, etc. When this occurs for one of your clients, your role is to be a steady guide through it. A good way to do this is to be the steady, predictable reference point for your client for a few minutes. Your confidence, comforting tone of voice, gentle comforting touch, pragmatic words, and ability to be calmly present are the keys to supporting your client in re-centering within their being. When your client becomes dramatic, your role is to become calmly pragmatic.

Supporting your client's personal power

Your client's wholeness belongs to them and they need to be able to maintain it on their own. In the work you do with them, support their autonomy, wisdom, and personal power. This is easy to do during sessions by teaching them skills that support their ongoing well-being and growth on all levels.

Here are some ideas that are easy to include in sessions:

♥ Verbally give your client permission to take good care of themselves and to be the final authority on their own life.

♥ Encourage your client to use language in ways that are empowering by using empowering language in your conversations with them. Directly teach them about empowering language when it feels appropriate to do so. Chapter 21 includes information about how to do this.

♥ Show your client how to recognize their body's truth about all aspects of their life.

♥ Introduce your client to some basic healing, nurturing, discernment, and personal growth skills such as:
  • Ways to massage areas of their body that are challenged.
  • How to touch their body in ways that move energy.
  • How to work with their solar plexus chakra.
  • Basic tarot, pendulum, or divination skills that help them look deeper into their own truths.

- Basic yoga or other forms of stretching that help their body, emotions, and mind, stay flexible.
- Simple grounding techniques and how to know when they're ungrounded.

One way to support your client's personal power as you end a session is to encourage them to trust their own wisdom about when or if it's time to work with you again. Even though this runs contrary to common wisdom about how to help your business thrive, I find that my clients appreciate this open door approach. With clients I've worked with before, instead of asking them about scheduling another appointment, I tell them it's been a pleasure working with them again. With first time clients, I say something to this effect: "So you'll know, the way I work with people is for you to take today's session home and let it settle in. Then trust yourself to know if or when it's time to work with me again. If that time comes, just get in touch with me."

Helping people expand their possibilities

You can do a lot to help your clients remember who they really are and how capable they really are.

Many people have frequent experiences that tell them they can't live in ways that support their well-being. As a result, they've forgotten that they're the center of their own life and can always make other choices. When this occurs, people often know more about what they don't want than what they do want.

Work with this by listening to what your client says and validating what you heard. Then offer them other possibilities for their consideration. Your client may reject quite a few of your suggestions. That's fine – what you're both looking for is the perfect fit for your client. Naming and eliminating things they don't align with will eventually reveal what they do align with.

Here are some other approaches that also work well:
- ♥ When your client says they don't know the next right step to take, or right decision to make, try one of these responses…
  - If you did know the answer, what do you imagine it would be?
  - If you don't know who does?
  - I'd like you to reword that this way, "Until now, I haven't known…"
- ♥ Help your client remember their inner roadmap by asking them to notice how their body feels when they align with their own wisdom. Give them permission to make their decisions based on how well a variety of options align with their own wisdom.

Here are the basics:

- "Yes"

    When "yes" is coming from our inner wisdom it feels right in every aspect of our being. This is a "yes" our wisdom is telling us to act on.

    When "yes" is coming from a desire to please, avoid conflict, or accomplish something, it feels useful, logical, or necessary. This is a "yes" we may want to consider more thoroughly before acting on it.

- "No"

    When "no" is coming from our inner wisdom it feels right in every aspect of our being. This is a "no" our wisdom is telling us to act on.

    When "no" is coming from our self-limitations it feels necessary, harsh, or we feel a desire to make excuses for it. This is a "no" we may want to grow beyond.

- "Maybe".

    When "maybe" is coming from our inner wisdom it feels right in every aspect of their being and it means now isn't the right time to make that particular decision or choice.

    When "maybe" is coming from avoidance or self-limitations it feels convenient, useful, or we feel a desire to avoid the topic. This is a "maybe" we may want to let go of by choosing "yes" or "no".

♥ When you see options your client doesn't see, present those options something like this, "Some ideas have come to me. I'm going to say them one at a time and I'd like you to let me know how your body responds to each possibility."

As you go through the list, affirm your client's wisdom by acknowledging that their response is their truth. Keep track of which options they have the most positive responses to. After you've gone through the whole list, help them explore their most positive responses a bit further.

Leave your client with hope and humor

Regardless of the nature or depth of challenges your client is living with, there are always gifts in those challenges and humor in some aspects of living with them. Among all the other things you do with your clients, look for these and gently share them when the moment feels right. It's ok for you and your client to laugh together and celebrate together during a session.

Working with Medical Conditions

For a variety of reasons, clients often come to healers about medical concerns. Due to the penalties for violating medical licensing laws, it's important that you know how to respect those laws and still do your work. Medical licensing laws in the United States and many other countries cover physical, psychiatric, and psychological conditions.

The definite legal line is usually that you have to be an appropriately licensed medical professional to make a diagnosis or prescribe medications. Exceptions to these laws do exist. In the United States, the exceptions are generally based on the religion or native tribal membership of both the healer and the client.

If you and your clients don't fit into one of those categories, here are some things you can legally do:

♥ Instead of prescribing a treatment, make suggestions such as:

"If I was dealing with that, I'd do this…"

"You might consider trying this…"

"You could check with your doctor and see if this is safe for you…"

♥ Instead of diagnosing, say things such as:

"Check with your doctor and see if this is true…"

"I don't know for sure, but you may be dealing with…"

"If I had that going on, I'd check to find out if it's…"

Medical licensing laws in the United States don't cover spiritual perspectives about the causes or purposes of medical conditions. They also don't cover nutritional consultations. If you do these types of work, make sure you have the necessary skills and then just do what you do.

In the United States, licensed ministers can legally provide counseling services, hands-on-healing, and spiritual support. Usually, the only legal requirement for ministerial licensing is that it has to be done through a church that's legally recognized by the state you work in. If you don't want to work with a local church, check online for churches that provide licensing.

Working with people who take pharmaceutical medications

Compared to people who don't use pharmaceuticals, the bodies of people who do use them are generally slower to respond to natural remedies, energywork, and bodywork. Be prepared for this and if needed, let your client know their body just requires some extra support.

Working with Challenging Clients

Challenging is different for each of us. When you feel that a client is challenging, check in with yourself and see if you want the type of challenge the client is offering you. If you want the challenge, view it as a growth opportunity and stick with it. If you don't want the challenge, please honor your own truth and step away from that client relationship.

Knowing your own limitations of tolerance for others will help greatly with discerning which challenges you can gracefully accept and which you'll respond to by taking yourself out of balance. Get clear about which types of behavior, attitudes, world views, expectations, requests, etc. you flow with gracefully. Get clear about which ones you resist, avoid as much as possible, have judgments about, or get caught up in. Don't judge yourself in any of this, just accept the truth of your own being and make your decisions based on that. When working with clients, being out of balance is not the face you want to present.

Please remember, you're not here to help everyone. You're here to help the people who align with your work. If you decide to end, or not begin, a client relationship that's challenging, let the person know in a polite, professional way and then move on.

Here are some ideas about how to do this:
- ♥ Tell them you're not the best healer for the challenges they're working with and offer suggestions about how to find someone who works well with their situation.
- ♥ Encourage them to expand their ability to support their own wholeness by working with the situation on their own for awhile. Give them information about ways to do that.

The ways clients are challenging sometimes include direct challenges to us. A good way to work with this is to stay emotionally detached, which is a foundation for relationships with all clients. Some challenges will be legitimate – you may have misspoken or overstepped a boundary. Respond to legitimate challenges calmly, honestly, and by taking responsibility for your part in the situation. Some challenges will be projections that are real for your client and are not real about you or about the relationship between the two of you. Respond to projected challenges honestly and calmly. If you want to end the session or conversation, do that politely and professionally.

Some ways clients may challenge us:
- ♥ Emotional outbursts.

When this occurs watch for a moment that feels right to you. When you find that moment, interrupt your client by calmly saying something to this effect, "I'd like you to pause here and breathe with me for a few seconds." Then demonstrate calm breathing by taking slow, deep inhales and exhales. Ask your client to breathe the same way. Repeat this as often as needed. Some people have learned to make sure they're heard or understood by being dramatic. What you're doing is teaching your client they'll be heard and understood by being calm.

♥ Requests that you prove your skills.

When this occurs, tell the person about your qualifications, training, certifications, or years of experience if that feels right to you. Beyond that, just move forward with seeing if they want to schedule a session. If this challenge occurs during a session, suggest that moving through the rest of the session will let them see what you can and can't do for them. If they want to end the session, end it. If they're dissatisfied at the end of the session, a good option is to gift the session to them and politely tell them it's important to feel aligned with the healer they're working with and encourage them to find a healer they feel more aligned with.

♥ Requests that you fix them or their situation.

When this occurs, tell your client that they're the only one who has the power to change their own life. You can give them suggestions, ideas, advice, remedies, etc.; and their job is to act on the information that resonates with them.

My Experience With This:

When I've given all the energy that's mine to give to a person or situation, I feel a slight push back or slight refusal to receive. It feels to me like the recipient is full. Within myself, my mind may begin to wander, I may feel bored with the situation, and it feels unproductive to continue focusing on the dynamic. I often know that if I do continue to participate, I'll be doing that to appease the other person rather than to contribute to their well-being or mine.

CHAPTER 7
WORKING WITH COUPLES & FAMILIES

Couples and families have intricately woven emotional dynamics that sometimes interfere with love, kindness, and clear communication. As a healer, your role in couple and family sessions often includes helping clients stay aligned with honesty, respect, and love for each other as they move through their healing process together.

Here are some ways to support this:

♥ Ask your clients to sit beside each other, or in a circle. This helps create team energy rather than oppositional energy.

♥ Encourage each person to learn, grow, process, and resolve at their own pace. And encourage each of the others to support that.

♥ When your clients are trying to resolve a challenge, keep the conversation on point.

♥ Teach your clients how to be sacred listeners. You can do this by asking one person to speak while the others listen silently and neutrally. Gently maintain this by reminding anyone who makes comments, makes sounds, interrupts, or shows an opinion through body language, that their only role right then is to be a sacred listener.

♥ As many times as needed during the session, give each person a chance to speak their truth while the others are their sacred listeners.

♥ Encourage your clients to talk to each other rather than about each other.

♥ Encourage your clients to look directly at each other when they're talking to each other.

♥ Remind your clients to take responsibility for their own words, actions, and emotions rather than blaming or crediting someone else.

♥ When your clients are unable to talk to each other, pause the conversation and encourage them to look at you and speak their truth to you while the others are their sacred listeners.

♥ If a conversation becomes angry, defensive, argumentative, or circular, ask everyone to pause, be silent, and breathe. Maintain this silent pause for about a minute. If needed, encourage one or more of them to step out of the room (separately) for a few minutes and regain their center.

♥ If needed, remind your clients that each of them holds part of the truth, none of them holds all of it, and their love is big enough to embrace their combined truth.

♥ Ask each person to look each of the others in the eye and say, "I love you." This can be done anytime, and as many times, as flows well with the session. Don't use this to defuse an intense situation when your clients are challenged with each other during the session. Instead, guide them through the challenge to a point where they're relating to each other more than they're relating to the challenge and then ask them to say, "I love you."

♥ Encourage full resolution of any challenges. If even one person feels unresolved, the situation is not resolved.

Some Techniques that Work Well with Couples and Families

Ancestral Lineage Healing

This is a guided meditation process and it can only be done when the client(s) actively participate. This is used to heal dysfunctional family dynamics that have come down through generations. This process can also be helpful when couples are challenged due to relationship expectations they carry from their childhoods. This process is described fully in Chapter 14.

Acknowledgements

Plan on 15 – 20 minutes for this process.

My instructions are oriented toward couples and can easily be adapted for use between any two beloveds.

This is an interactive process that can only be done when both partners are participating. Each partner has a turn speaking and a turn receiving. This way of acknowledging each other helps couples see each other more clearly, learn more about each other, and actively appreciate what each partner does to support their life together.

If your clients need help getting started, here are some examples of things to acknowledge: going to work each day, making our home comfortable, enjoying my mom, your willingness to listen to me, enjoying my creativity, rubbing my feet, enjoying my body, being a great dad to our kids, loving our dog, filling my car with gas the other day…

I recommend doing this once during a session so the couple understands how to do it. Then ask them to do this at home at least once weekly for as long as it feels right to them. Instructions for couples to use at home are in Section 6 – Self-Guided Healing Techniques.

Acknowledgements Process

Ask your clients to sit facing each other, preferably on comfortable seating that allows them to touch each other with no barriers between them. Ask them to decide which of them will speak first and which will listen first. Then give them the following instructions one step at a time as they move through the process.

1. To the listener:
   - Listen silently and just absorb what your beloved is saying. Don't comment or ask for explanations. Just receive.
2. To the speaker:
   - One thing at a time, tell your beloved what you see her/him doing that supports your love and your life together. Before each item, please say, "I acknowledge you for…"
3. When the speaker stops or indicates that's all they want to say:
   - Ask your beloved if she/he received these acknowledgements.
4. If the listener hasn't received the acknowledgements:
   - The speaker then asks if she/he would like anything to be repeated or would like a moment to absorb what was said.
5. When the listener has received the acknowledgements:
   - The speaker then asks if she/he would like to be acknowledged for anything more.
6. If the listener wants to be acknowledged for more:
   - To the speaker: Simply acknowledge your beloved for anything she/he says. Don't debate, question, or ask for an explanation.
   - To the listener: One thing at a time, say what else you want to be acknowledged for, pausing after each thing so your beloved can give you the acknowledgement.
7. When this is complete, ask the couple to switch roles and do steps 1 - 6 again.
8. After both partners have spoken and listened, ask them to finish by sharing a warm hug and "I love you."

CHAPTER 8
WORKING WITH GROUPS

The same basic concepts used for individual sessions apply to classes, healing circles, and group sessions. The main difference with groups is that you'll also need to keep everyone focused and moving along together. Group work can include any number of people you're comfortable with and have the physical space to accommodate. I find that having at least 5 people involved keeps the energy moving easily. Large groups work best when the focus is kept on the entire group or when individual attention is provided by guiding everyone into group activities of 2 – 4 people who will focus on each other for short periods of time.

In your planning:
♥ Keep the session to 2 hours or less, or build in some breaks.
♥ Have some idea about how long you'd like to focus on each person or activity. Make this a bit flexible so you can move with the group dynamic as things progress.
♥ If more than one person will be speaking, on plan enough time for each person to be heard.
♥ In case the group wants to explore one part of your plan more deeply, be prepared to let go of other parts.
♥ In case the group doesn't connect with one part of your plan, be prepared to include something else, go deeper into something else, or let the session end a bit early.
♥ If you'll be doing healing work in a circle, leave open spaces at opposite points in the perimeter of the circle so there are paths for energy and spirit helpers to freely come and go. One way to do this is to leave an opening at each direction – North, South, East, and West.

When you begin the group session:
♥ Explain basic etiquette for the session. Here are some things to consider:
   ● This is sacred space and confidentiality is expected – what happens here stays here.
   ● Please don't interrupt.
   ● Please don't have side conversations.
   ● Please be a sacred witness to each person's process.
   ● Cell phones and other devices are off and ignored during the session.
   ● If you need to take a break, please silently leave the room and silently return when you're ready.

As you move through the session:

♥ Check in from time to time to make sure everyone can hear you.

♥ Watch for boredom, yawning, or side interactions. If you notice any of this, pick up the pace a bit, ask everyone to stand up and stretch or move around, call a break, or shift what the group is doing to something that requires active physical participation for a few minutes.

♥ Watch the group etiquette and if needed, gently re-engage participants in the basic etiquette you established.

Ideas for this:

- A gentle touch
- A direct, respectful request such as, "Please hold that to yourself while we complete this." Then after "this" is complete, return to the person and ask if they still want some attention about whatever it was.
- Catch the person's eye and silently make a subtle, calming motion with your hands.
- Pause for a second and, without focusing on any particular person, say something like, "Please continue silently being sacred witnesses to…"

♥ Give each person your full attention from time to time.

♥ It there are more than four people and group conversation is included, use a talking symbol. This can be a stick, flower, stone, or any other object that's unique and easy to pass around the group. While a person is holding the talking symbol, they're the only one who can speak.

Some people speak concisely and some speak in long, winding stories. It's up to you to make sure there's enough time for each person to speak and to be heard. It's also up to you to move the conversation forward when someone wanders off point or takes too much time.

Here are some ways to do that:

- At the beginning of the speaking time, ask the whole group to speak as concisely as possible to make sure everyone has time to be heard.
- Watch the time and let each speaker know when they have about one minute left.
- When someone speaks for too long, gently interrupt them and remind them that everyone needs a chance to talk and it's time for them to complete what they're saying.

Healing Circles

Focuses can include anything of interest to you and those attending. Healing circles are held for individuals, groups, Earth, loved ones in spirit, animals, whole species, widespread human dynamics such as war, racism, poverty, etc.

Some techniques that work well in healing circles:

- ♥ Reiki
- ♥ Guided meditation
- ♥ Ritual
- ♥ Creating something together
- ♥ Dance
- ♥ Singing, drumming, etc.
- ♥ Massage

  Several people massaging one person at the same time.

  -or-

  Sitting in a circle and everyone massaging the person in front of them at the same time.
- ♥ Sharing

  Each person has time to share their heart and receive responses from the rest of the circle.

  -or-

  Each person has time in the center of the circle while all others focus on giving them healing through touch, thought, energy, or ritual.
- ♥ Individual healing – the circle is focused on one person and all others are there to support that one. This can be especially beneficial when someone is

seriously ill, grieving, or needs a lot of loving support for any reason.

Contact Improvisation

This is a free style partner dance that can be done with or without music. It has no established steps or movements and requires no experience or confidence with dance. The focus of this activity is on the quality of contact and presence with each other.

Contact Improv helps us remember how to be creative, flexible, and harmonious in our interactions with others. It helps expand our ease with the unknown and our awareness of our own comfort zones about touching and being touched. It also helps us learn how to do what we want to do while respecting, appreciating, and supporting what another person wants to do.

If more than five people participate, it's easiest to dance if they're divided into groups of five or less.

Here are the basics:

♥ With the partners keeping physical contact between their bodies, the dance is done any way they want to do it. The point of contact can change as they move, they just can't completely lose contact with each other's body.

Example: The partners begin dancing by touching finger tips, then one touches their hip to the other's leg, while waiting to break the fingertip contact until they've established the hip to leg contact and their partner has accepted that by allowing it.

♥ Every partner leads and none follows.
♥ The movement in this dance can constant or it can wander in and out of periods when one or more partners stays still.
♥ The dance continues until one partner is ready to stop dancing.

Search online to see videos of Contact Improvisation.

Wisdom Circles
This is a way to support everyone in doing a little teaching and learning by sharing their own insights, questions, perspectives and wisdoms. After you get the conversation rolling, invite participants to share what they know, perceive, have questions about, etc. When the conversation slows down keep the group energy flowing by asking who'd like to speak next or by bringing in a new topic. I find this to be a delightful way to share healing skills and spiritual insights.

Full Body Fascial Unwinding
Minimum of 6 participants, 7 is ideal.
Plan on 2 – 4 hours.
It's helpful to have drinking water and light snacks available for everyone.

This process enhances flexibility, creativity, body/mind connection, emotional clarity, and it's a lot of fun. For a person who has limited physical strength or agility, this also provides an opportunity to physically move in ways they're unable to do on their own.

This is usually done on the floor – hard surface, large area rugs, or fully carpeted floors are best. To avoid tripping don't use throw rugs, blankets, cushions, or pillows. This can be done on a massage table, just be careful to keep the table steady as everyone moves around. The space needs to be big enough and clear enough of obstacles for the group to move safely and freely. If the space is big enough, multiple groups can do this at the same time.

If desired, each person has a turn to be in the middle with five people supporting them. If there are seven participants, one person relaxes and grounds, helps the group avoid bumping into obstacles as they're moving, and if needed gives a support person a break.

It's normal for each person who's unwinding to be in the process for anywhere from 5 – 45 minutes.

Basic process for Full Body Fascial Unwinding:

1. The person who'll be unwinding lays on their back on the floor.

2. The guiding support person: Sitting on the floor at the top of the person's head, use both hands to gently cradle their head.

3. The other 4 support people: Sitting on the floor, space themselves around the person who's unwinding, each supporting one arm or leg by gently holding it on the palms of both hands.

4. The guiding support person: Remind the person who's unwinding to ask for what they want or need at any time during the process, to move in any way that feels right to them, and to make any sounds they want to.

    Then begin the process by asking the person to close their eyes and keep them closed, breathe gently, and begin moving in any way they want to whenever they're ready.

    ♥ If the person doesn't start moving within a minute or so, here are some gentle, spoken suggestions to help them:
    - Check in with your body. Is there a finger or toe that wants to move? Maybe an eyelid?
    - Would you like to wiggle, roll, or shift position?
    - Would any part of your body be more comfortable if you moved it a bit?

5. From here, all the support people keep supporting the weight of the person's legs, arms, torso, or head. If needed, they can shift to other areas of the person's body as the unwinding evolves.

6. Unless the person who's unwinding asks you to do so, don't suggest, guide, push, or try to position them. Just let their body do what it does and simply support their movements. They may roll, lay still, move one part of their body, sit up, stand up, bend, twist, ask to be held or stretched, etc. Just keep supporting them and moving with them without controlling or directing their movements.

7. At some point, the person who's unwinding will lay still for awhile. When this happens, the guiding person asks something to this effect, "Please check in with yourself and see if you want to move more."

    ♥ If yes, keep going for however long the person wants to move. Then ask again.

♥   If no, stay in a circle around them and ask them to sit up when they're ready and open their eyes. When they're ready, help them to their feet, walk them to a chair, and give them a glass of water.

8. Before beginning with the next person, give everyone a few minutes to refresh themselves.

One of My Favorite Stories About Working With Groups

A friend of mine was confined to a psychiatric hospital against her wishes and for reasons she felt were an attempt to prevent her from pursuing legal action against a man who'd abused her. Several of her other friends and I held a healing circle for her, sending energetic support to her whole being to regain balance. We also asked for help from everyone on the spirit side who was willing and able to wisely guide the doctors into releasing her as soon as that supported her well-being. Two days later she called to tell us she was home and doing fine. What started out to be a thirty-day hospital stay transformed into four days and successful legal action against the man who'd abused her.

CHAPTER 9
MAINTAINING YOUR WHOLENESS

Showing up as someone who holds compassionate, healthy boundaries provides others with a living example of one of the foundation blocks for their own empowerment – deciding what they will and won't participate in.

Healthy, compassionate boundaries come from within you and are about your own behavior. They originate in your sense of integrity and the wisdom of your own body and soul. They guide you in making decisions that support your own well-being and the well-being of others. They show up in your loving and firm "no" to things that don't interest you or are detrimental to your well-being. They're your awareness of when it's really ok with you to set aside your desires or needs for the good of another. They're your ability to ask for what you need and your enthusiastic "yes" to things that interest you or align with your well-being. The most sustainable boundaries are strong enough to maintain your access to your own wisdom and flexible enough to integrate life's surprises.

Honoring Your Personal Needs and Preferences

Decide where and how working as a healer fits into your life
Give yourself the gift of choosing how your work as a healer needs to flow with the rest of your life. You're not here to sacrifice your own quality of life for the well-being of others. You're here to show everyone how to do the work they do in the world and enjoy a delightful, fulfilling life at the same time.

My Experience With This:
Early in my work as a healer, I offered a few minutes of healing to almost everyone who I noticed could benefit from it. I enjoyed it and it gave me a lot of experience working quickly with a variety of people in settings ranging from noisy crowded gathering places to quiet one-on-one visits. As part of my learning process, this was a valuable experience. As an ongoing way of being a healer, it was unsustainable.

Have inspiring interests other than healing
Healers focus on the things that are out of balance because that's where our work is. When this is our only inspiring interest, we eventually see the imbalances in life more readily than we see the beauty and perfection. That will wear anyone down. Keep yourself inspired and delighted with life by also having interests that take your mind completely away from the imbalances and immerse you fully in all that's beautiful and perfect here on Earth.

Work in environments you enjoy

Whether you have your own healing space or you share space with others, you're in full control of the environment you work in. Choose locations or a location that are easy for you to access, provide the privacy and quiet you want with clients, and support your physical and emotional health. Be sure the location helps you stay centered and you love sharing it with clients.

Work with clients you enjoy

At some point in your work as a healer, you'll probably encounter some clients you'd prefer not to work with. Regardless of your reasons for not wanting to work with someone, it really is ok to be choosy about your clients and to be choosy about the types of challenges you're willing to work with.

While you can't always know if you align with a client before you work with them, at the end of a session you can respectfully refer them to another healer. A way to do this is to politely tell them you've completed what you know how to do for them and if they'd like additional support, you'll be happy to give them contact information for other healers. Be sure you have contact information readily available in a form you can give to your client – business cards, website info, or a paper with names and phone numbers.

My Experience With This:
I believed for awhile that my work was primarily with a small variety of living humans. I wanted to work with people of a certain world view, I didn't want to work with people who had died, and I thought working with any other species required skills I didn't have. After a couple of years of that, I was bored and frustrated and not at all sure I wanted to continue being a healer. When I opened my mind to working with anyone who found their way to me, I found the core of myself as a healer and I've loved my work ever since. My choice of clients began as a select few and grew to include almost everyone.

Work in ways you enjoy

Being aware of your interests and passions will help you discover your natural alignment as a healer. With that alignment, you'll do your best work. Use modalities you're enthusiastic about. Work with situations and challenges you feel inspired about helping to heal. A big part of being a healer is facilitating wholeness in our clients' lives. When we're a living example of being aligned with ourselves, we offer clients proof that wholeness is within their reach.

My Experience With This:

Early in my work as a healer, I worked with anything anyone brought my way. That was ok until I realized there were some situations and dynamics that I was consistently impatient with. I could put on the appearance of unconditional love and acceptance in the presence of anyone I worked with, but I wasn't always feeling it within myself. I didn't like that. I knew other healers who really lit up when they worked with those situations and dynamics and I couldn't understand why I couldn't just step up and authentically do it too.

When I finally heard my own self-judgement, and for lack of any other ideas about how to feel better about myself, I gave myself a little slack for not being perfect. That's when I accidentally remembered I'm one of many, many healers and the only "right" way to be a healer is to do what I do best.

Work within your skills

It's good for you and your clients when you know and honor your own chosen focus and your limitations and preferences. Please don't try to be everything to everyone – some situations are not yours to work with.

When the situation or timing doesn't fit, give yourself permission to make referrals or to tell the person you can't work with their situation. When someone wants something you don't want to give or has issues you don't want to work with, again, give yourself permission to make referrals or tell the person you can't work with their situation.

When you have the needed skills and you're uncomfortable working with the client or the situation, trust your wisdom about how to respond. Sometimes it's best to refuse the session or refer the client to someone else. Sometimes it's best to give yourself the opportunity to gain confidence by working with the situation.

Work in ways that support your belief system and respect your clients' belief systems

It's ok to use your world view, religion, spiritual practice, or personal preferences as foundations for your work as a healer. It's also ok to express some of that in sessions. It's not ok to push those things on your clients.

If your belief system includes a perspective that your way is the right way, or that it's your responsibility to bring others into that way of living, please remember… that type of interaction is not the work of a healer – it's the work of an activist or an evangelist. If you're unable to fully appreciate and respect the ways of others, please do healing work exclusively with people who already align with your belief system.

Work in ways that support your personal time and space

In addition to meeting the needs and availability of clients, your business hours need to provide you with the time you want for self-care, family, and enjoyment of life. Choose business hours that work for you and change them as needed to continue supporting your own well-being in all ways. Protect your time off – you need time away from your work to keep yourself fresh and ready to be present to clients.

Sometimes clients will act as if their desire or need for your services is more urgent or important than anything else in your life. It's up to you to know the difference between a situation that requires your immediate attention and a situation that is better addressed at another time or by someone else. Agree to work with clients only when you can be fully present to them and give them your undivided attention and healing skills without any concern that you're neglecting something else.

If you work in your home, choose which parts of the house and property your clients can enjoy and which are private. In ways that are unobtrusive to you and are also obvious, be sure your clients know which spaces are theirs to enjoy.

Decide if, or when, you're willing to welcome clients into your personal world. Some clients will feel personally connected with you, or you'll feel that with them. If both of you want a personal connection and are able to stay clear about what's personal and what's business, it's fine to expand the relationship. If you prefer to keep the two separate, be clear about that with yourself and any clients who meander toward your personal life.

Balancing your professional skills in your personal relationships

As wonderful as our skills with healing, empathy, and intuition are, focusing too much of this on our loved ones can really diminish the quality of those relationships. This is especially true with a spouse/partner, close relatives, and close friends. Because of our healing skills we sometimes see options for them that they don't see. Because of our emotional connection we can easily misinterpret our intuitive insights about them. Because of the frequency and intensity of contact between us, our loved ones can feel suffocated, controlled, or under the microscope.

Be kind to your loved ones by relating to them based on what actually occurs between the two of you. Be the compassionate, insightful, loving person you are. At the same time respect their expertise about their own life as much as you respect your own.

Keeping Your Energy Clear

First and most importantly, make space for your clients to release their excess energy directly to the earth or sky without passing it through you. Do this by giving yourself permission to be emotionally detached from their process. It's fine to touch, hug, empathize, or encourage a client during a release, just stay clear within yourself that the energy they release is returning directly from them to the earth or sky.

Know yourself and your body

It's important to know you well enough to know when you've absorbed someone else's excess energy. Signs that you've absorbed something from a client usually appear during the session or within the first hour after the session. In your body, heart, or mind they'll feel sudden, unfamiliar, out of place, or without a known cause. Some signs that you've absorbed someone else's energy:
- ♥ Unfamiliar aches and pains in your body
- ♥ Headache
- ♥ Confusion
- ♥ Mood change
- ♥ Digestive issues

If you notice any of this, some simple ways to re-balance yourself include smudging all the way around your body, taking a shower with the intention that you're releasing the energy, or sitting with your back against a tree while you allow the tree to absorb the energy.

Know when to heal you

Give yourself permission to know when a client's imbalance has revealed something or your own that's ready to be healed. Signs this has occurred usually appear during the session or within the first twenty-four hours after the session. When this happens, take advantage of it by healing that aspect of yourself after the session ends and as soon as you have time to lovingly tend to you.

Some signs that a client's imbalance has revealed your own opportunity to heal:
- ♥ Emotional or mental pull to be alone or to focus within yourself
- ♥ Your old memories or emotions coming to the surface
- ♥ Confusion about yourself
- ♥ Agitation about your emotions
- ♥ Working with multiple clients in a short period of time who all request healing for the same type of issue

Let others hold their own pain stories

This is an essential skill for healers. We can easily become the museum, or library, for the pain stories of everyone on the planet. We notice these stories through sessions with clients, encounters with friends and family, media, and ordinary life tasks we do within our communities. No one can stay balanced if they hold all of the pain stories they notice.

Being a sacred witness and compassionate presence to others is a natural for healers and when we do that in healthy ways, it's beneficial for everyone. Please choose health with this – listen, empathize, take action to alleviate the pain when and how you can, and don't use another's pain story to generate pain within yourself. Use the pain stories you're aware of to generate your own creative thinking so you can help heal the root source of the pain. That level of healing releases everyone from any future need to experience that type of pain.

Before you begin each session

It's helpful to set the rest of your life aside for the duration of the session. Your client deserves your undivided attention and your work will be higher quality when you're fully present.

At the very least, do these things:

♥ Before a session begins, finish any tasks that will distract your focus.
♥ Give yourself permission to ignore things going on outside of the session.
♥ Turn off your phone and any other communication devices.

After each session

It's a good idea to re-center in your own energy before you do another session or engage in other activities. Usually this can be done by having a drink of water, taking a few seconds of intentional breathing, taking a short walk, or by holding a grounding stone such as hematite, smoky quartz, or a pebble from your yard.

Some sessions will linger in your heart or mind. Some will have an emotional impact on you. Some will ignite your imagination and invite further exploration. When you feel this type of connection with a session you've done for someone else, you're being invited to see how the session applies to your own life. These clear invitations to learn about aspects of yourself are one of the benefits of being a healer.

After a session that catches your attention like this, it's good to close your connection to the person you worked with by returning to your center in a more physical way than you normally do. This will create a strong distinction between the information and energy that belongs to the person you worked with and the information and energy that belongs to you.

Some ways you can do this type of centering:

♥ Smudge yourself using sage or incense
♥ Play a hand drum while passing it around your body.
♥ Take a shower with the intention that you're releasing all that isn't yours.
♥ Dance or shake your body with the intention that you're releasing all that isn't yours.
♥ Stand outside for awhile with your bare feet solidly on the ground.
♥ Give yourself an hour or more to focus on something other than your connection to the session.

When you're centered in yourself again, meditate or do a reading asking what in you is ready to come to consciousness as a result of your experience in that session. Be with this question gently. The answer will come to your conscious mind in its own timing, which may be immediate or may be when you're in a situation in which the information is helpful.

Periodically clear and balance the energy in your healing space. Here are some ways to do that:

♥ Open all the windows and doors for 5 – 10 minutes and let fresh air fill the space.
♥ Smudge the space with sage or incense.
♥ Place a clear quartz cluster in the center of the space and leave it there for a couple of days.
♥ Chant, sing, tone, drum, or pray in a way that feels clearing and balancing to you.

When people put you on a pedestal

This happens sometimes, especially when you're really skilled at what you do. This may show up as people wanting to be like you or wanting to be around more than you want them to be. It may show up as people speaking as if you're superior to them or a necessary part of their life. They may emulate you in some way or get upset when you display your own humanity. Regardless of how this shows up, remember that you're not a healer so you can gather followers, you're a healer so you can support people in living their own version of wholeness. Stay centered in your own integrity and don't participate in the stories and perceptions about who other people want you to be or who they think you are.

Keeping Yourself Fresh in Your Work

As the years go by, some aspects of your work as a healer will become routine. This can be good when it comes to the frame of your work – the ways you move through sessions, your tried and true professional techniques, your marketing approach, your bookkeeping… Routine can become burdensome when you get bored with it, feel like you're in a rut, or rely on the same technique for every session. All of these are signs that it's time to shake things up a bit so you can continue to be inspired and enthusiastic about the work you do.

Notice your own boredom and what you're bored with. Decide if it's time for you to learn something new, let go of some part of your business, take a vacation, shift your professional focus a bit… Break up the routine in some way that pleases you.

Notice your professional ruts – those places where your work lacks creativity or innovative responses. Add some sparkle to these areas by doing things differently. Rearrange your office furniture, or the way you conduct sessions. Meet clients outdoors for awhile, learn a new skill or add a new dynamic to a skill you already have… Give yourself permission to be a little less predictable in the context of your work.

Notice when you don't want to work during your normal business hours. Shorten or lengthen your hours, shift your hours around a bit so you can do other things during some times or days that you were working, take a day or a week off. Give yourself some flexibility to find your next right business schedule.

When You're Exhausted by It All…

… and you will be from time to time. Regardless of how resilient, strong, self-nurturing, or enthusiastic you are, there will be times when being aware of the imbalances in the world feels like a heavy burden. This is normal. When you feel this, give yourself a break. Take time away from clients, from dreamtime work, from studying, from the news. Take a break from everything that keeps you aware of what's out of balance in yourself or the world. For a few days, hours, or weeks fill your time with things you really enjoy doing; things that deeply nurture and relax your whole being. Play and let life fill you up until you're overflowing again.

SECTION 3

SKILL DEVELOPMENT

I explore what inspires me.

CHAPTER 10
CHOOSING MODALITIES AND TEACHERS

It's important to follow your own interests and passions when deciding what you want to learn and how you want to interact with those you'll be helping. The modalities, techniques and ways of interacting that you most enjoy are the ones that you naturally align with. Having this natural alignment will enhance all that you do as a healer.

Choosing Your Modalities

Your skills and perspective as a healer will be broader and more flexible if you learn several modalities. If you don't already know which modalities you'd like to start with, read about a variety of them and what's required to use them proficiently. Before taking any formal training in a new modality, have at least one session with someone who offers that type of work. Experiencing it yourself will help you know if that way of healing or growing resonates with you enough for you to enjoy offering it to clients.

If you're new to seeing yourself as a healer, it's helpful to take at least a few classes in a modality you like. This will help you understand how to design sessions and interact with those you'll be helping. It will also provide you with perspective about your skills and give you some ideas for developing them further. If you want to earn your living as a healer, it's helpful to become certified in at least one modality.

The training for some holistic modalities is very expensive in terms of time and money; others are very affordable. Be practical when you decide what to learn and also follow your truth by honoring your interests, financial resources, and timing regarding the learning process.

Licensing

Some state and local governments require licensing for some or all holistic healing modalities. If you live in an area with licensing requirements for any of your chosen modalities, getting licensed is easier than dealing with the legal ramifications and marketing restrictions that come with being unlicensed.

Choosing Your Teachers

Learning from a variety of teachers and in a variety of ways will give you a broad foundation of knowledge and perspective. Choosing teachers from a variety of cultures and approaches will provide a richness to your work that supports both you and your clients.

Consider how you learn most easily and choose teachers with styles that support those ways of learning. Do you learn best by being gently guided into new adventures? By being pushed to confront your fears, confusion, and stories? Do you learn best on your own? With the help or companionship of others? Do you learn best through information? Through experience? Through a combination of both?

My Experience With This:

My focus is on effective results that are inspiring and sustainable in my clients' lives; I keep that front and center. To help myself be the best healer I'm capable of being, I've chosen to experience a large variety of teachers from different cultures and backgrounds. I also choose ways to learn that I can easily afford in terms of time, energy, and money. I find the greatest value in the core concepts behind specific perspectives and techniques. I often look deeper into those core concepts and find my own ways to work with them. With each teacher, I keep the parts of their teachings that make sense to me and I let go of the rest. I trust that if I ever need any of the teachings I let go of, I'll remember them or find them again.

How Much Formal Training is Enough?

Being familiar with a lot of different techniques is very beneficial and formal training isn't always necessary. You can learn the basics about most holistic modalities by reading books or receiving sessions from other healers. You can develop your skills in many modalities by experimenting in your own life, participating in healing circles, or by practicing with friends, family, or others who are learning.

Take formal trainings to learn your foundation modality and anything else you need to meet certification or licensing requirements. Take formal trainings to become certified in any trademarked modalities you want to offer. Beyond that, take formal trainings when you have the interest, time, and money to do so without creating imbalances in your own life. Creating imbalances in your own life doesn't enhance your work as a healer.

Reading Your Own Signals About Right Direction

Notice, believe, and follow your enthusiasm – it shows you the directions you really want to go. Let your neutrality be neutral – it tells you to pause that decision until you can see it more clearly. Honor your resistance – it's a natural signal to go another direction. Notice what you admire about healers you've met or heard about – admiration shows you what you value.

If you're not certain you've accurately read your internal signals, use this simple technique to confirm what's real for you:

1. Begin by sitting quietly, breathing gently, and allowing yourself to come to center.

2. Then focus your attention on your solar-plexus chakra and ask your body to show you a "yes". Pay attention to your body's response to this question. Whatever that response is, that's your body's "yes" response to the questions that will follow.

3. Take a deep gentle breath – this will restore your attention to being fully present in the current moment.

4. Then focus your attention on your solar plexus and ask yourself a yes/no question about one of the options you're considering.
    Example: Is this a good teacher for me?

5. Pay attention to your body's response to that idea. If your body's response isn't "yes", that option isn't for you or isn't for you at this time.

6. Take another deep gentle breath, returning your attention to being fully present in the current moment.

7. Then ask your next question and notice your body's response.

8. Continue this process of taking a deep gentle breath, asking your next question, and noticing your body's response until you feel full for the time being or you've asked all of your current questions.

CHAPTER 11
INTUITIVE FLUENCY

The Importance of Intuition in Healing

Skillful healing often includes being able to gracefully figure out how to work with situations that are outside your realm of experience or knowledge. This includes exploring possibilities outside of your established process, expectations, and perspectives. It includes looking beyond perceived reality to see what else is possible and being aware that the illogical or unbelievable may be exactly what's true or needed in some situations. While intuitive fluency isn't necessary for healers, it's a very useful skill to have and I use it throughout every session.

Intuitive Awareness is Natural

Being intuitively wide awake and fully connected with spirit is normal for all people. We're born with the ability to simultaneously focus in both the spiritual and physical planes. Being closed off from this type of awareness is as unnatural as not being able to notice an itch somewhere on your own body.

Life experience is the difference between people who aren't aware this way and those who are. As we move through life some people choose to focus primarily on the physical plane, some focus primarily on the physical plane due to family or cultural dynamics, and some maintain or redevelop their simultaneous focus in both planes. At any time, anyone can choose to ignore one plane or the other or to embrace their ability to focus in both.

Full intuitive awareness comes from noticing all that's actually present in any given moment. This includes the obvious and all that fills the spaces between the obvious. In those spaces between the obvious are thoughts and feelings being expressed without words or actions, beings living in non-physical forms, information shared through activities and sounds, shifts in the energies surrounding us, and all else that we tend to overlook or see as irrelevant, beyond our capacity to understand, or imaginary.

Receiving intuitive insights is done by paying attention to the subtle information we often overlook, dismiss, or minimize. Learning to quickly and clearly understand that information is done by developing the skills of noticing on all levels and thinking outside of familiar patterns. When you do this as a normal part of your daily interactions, your intuitive awareness flows easily and naturally. It's as effortless as breathing.

The ability to clearly think into places where you have no foundation of knowledge or experience is a skill that strengthens by developing both your imagination and your ability to connect your imagination with observation and experience. These are the foundations of well-developed intuition. If you're not already accustomed to thinking this way, be patient with yourself, with practice you'll remember how to do this.

My Experience With This

I often think in what I call "two minds"; I'm consciously aware of two distinctly different areas of my brain working at the same time. Physically, this feels like one eye and one ear are fully present in the current physical moment, aware of all that I'm doing and all that's occurring in my environment. The other eye and ear are lightly present in the current physical moment while fully perceiving information from sources that aren't physical. Within me this feels just like multi-tasking – being fully grounded and functioning adeptly with a variety of things at the same time.

Intuition and Psychic Awareness Are the Same Thing

The only difference between them is that some people think there's a difference. People who consciously use intuitive awareness as often as they use their other normally functioning senses tend to be labeled psychic. People who use intuitive awareness unconsciously or infrequently tend to be labeled intuitive. Which word you use to describe your skills and experience is totally up to you.

My Experience With This

I prefer the word "intuitive" because I like the sound of the word and because so many people think psychics spend most of their time talking with people who've died. Among the many ways I work as a healer and live as an intuitively awake person, I do talk with people who've died. And that's a very small part of what I do.

Intuition, Imagination, and Logic

Intuition is an inborn skill that we naturally, and often unconsciously, use to guide ourselves through unknown experiences. It includes aspects of creative and logical thinking and thrives in the connection between them. Using imagination, intuitive awareness expands into what has yet to become known. Using logic, intuitive insights are grounded into what can be experienced on the physical plane.

Wondering is one of the most practical tools you have for expanding your intuitive awareness. Noticing what's going on in your thoughts and in the physical space around you, and wondering how those things might be connected to the information you're opening to receive, often brings unexpected insights that are spot on. Wondering this way isn't a long process. It's a very quick acknowledgement that things might be connected, followed by you giving your mind permission to consciously discover if they are.

My Experiences With This

Regardless of what I'm doing, I give myself permission to notice anything around me that catches my attention in an unusual way. My internal distinction is that if I notice and move on, it's normal. If I notice and want to experience more, or wish I hadn't noticed, it's unusual. When it's unusual, I pause for just a second and give myself permission to know why that stood out to me at that time. Then I move on and let the experience wander through my mind until the answer comes.

Neutrality and Openness

Imagination and logic can also cloud your interpretation of intuitive information and this is where it's important to have well-developed discernment skills. The combination of neutrality and openness is the best thing you can give yourself when you're intuitively alert. That combination will help you feel and know the difference between insights you're misinterpreting and insights you're accurately understanding.

One way to teach yourself to be neutral and open is to notice your emotional and physical responses to your intuitive experiences. Experiences and insights received with neutrality and openness land in your being very matter-of-factly. When you have emotional responses to these experiences it's because they've touched parts of you that need some loving attention. Perhaps that's an emotional wound, a hope, or a fear. Maybe the intuitive experience contradicts or validates a belief, judgment, value, or perspective of yours. Maybe it touched a deep loneliness or longing… Whatever it is, gently tend to the things behind your emotional responses.

This doesn't mean it's not ok for you to become emotionally engaged with your intuitive experiences and insights. We all do that at times. This is simply about giving yourself the skills that help you fully and accurately understand those experiences and insights.

My Experience With This

Early in my process of developing my intuitive skills, I wanted to channel insights that quickly and profoundly change humanity for the better. When I received a little glimpse of that kind of information, I got very excited and wrote it down to keep for the book I intended to write. I'd then put my notes away for days or weeks before re-reading them. When I re-read them, I often discovered that most of those new insights were based on perspectives of my own that I needed to grow beyond.

In those experiences, I was accurate in my interpretation that I'm capable of receiving and communicating insights that can profoundly change humanity. I was a bit short on catching the rest of the message until quite some time later. One part I initially missed is that I too am still learning how to be a fully loving person in some of the experiences I encounter on this physical plane. Another part is that the insights I receive are only part of the story and they have to be combined with the insights received by others. The final part is that changing humanity won't happen in my timing, it will happen when each human being chooses to embrace the insights that resonate with their own soul.

These experiences were a big lesson for me about the importance of setting aside my own agendas and perspectives so I'm able to fully understand the messages I receive.

Intuition and Mental Illness

In cultures that encourage mindful living, the combination of logic and creativity is viewed as complete thinking, while logic alone or creativity alone is viewed as incomplete thinking. In those cultures, easily accessed intuitive awareness is the norm and it's seen as just another skill that helps people understand life and move through it well.

In our modern and industrialized cultures, logical thinking is typically preferred and many of us adapt to that by ignoring or silencing creative and intuitive thoughts. When we start noticing or expressing them again, it's pretty common to go through a period of wondering if we're losing touch with reality. I assure you that if you didn't have a mental illness before you started developing your intuitive skills, you won't develop a mental illness by accessing your intuitive skills. Please trust yourself.

Also in our modern and industrialized cultures, we typically don't learn how to work with our intuition in childhood. As a result, people who stay intuitively open through childhood are sometimes diagnosed with mental illnesses or emotional disorders. In these situations, the imbalances are actually due to the combined stress of not knowing how to turn off their intuition when desired, having their perceptions either invalidated or not validated, and being taught to fear what they perceive. For people in this situation, learning to use their intuition with clarity often heals their "mental illness".

Intuitive Wisdom and Experiential Wisdom

The difference between intuitive wisdom and experiential wisdom is simple. Intuitive wisdom is based on future evidence and experiential wisdom is based on prior evidence.

Combining the two brings greater depth and practicality to your work as a healer. In wholeness, our logical, experience based thinking and our creative, intuitive based thinking work with each other and help us respond well to all that we encounter in life.

Logic helps us stay grounded on the physical plane. It's based experiences that have been lived and the known results of those experiences. Creativity helps us stay grounded on the spiritual plane. It's based on possibilities and unknown or potential results. The combination of logic and creativity helps us use practical and already known information in both familiar and innovative ways. It also helps us think into the unknown, intangible, or unproven and bring what we find there into lived experiences on the physical plane.

Protection

A lot of people believe receiving intuitive insights and doing spiritual journeys are dangerous activities unless you protect yourself from the evil or malicious beings and entities who hang out in the non-physical realm. The truth is that everything and everyone is working for the highest good of all, even when you don't yet understand how it all fits together.

There are no evil or malicious beings or entities. Just the same as occurs on the physical plane, some folks on the spiritual plane are frustrated and express that by being withdrawn, unkind, angry, aggressive, or demanding. These types of behavior are indications of an imbalance within the one behaving that way. If you encounter someone who's demonstrating imbalance, the most constructive response is to be a healer for them by being a gentle, loving presence in response to their challenges. Those living in the non-physical realm will always respond to this within a short time by restoring their own balance and expressing the loving soul they actually are.

It's not natural for people to be afraid to connect directly with those living on the spiritual plane. The spiritual plane, the non-physical realm, is our home. We came from there and we'll return there when our life here comes to completion.

Familiarity, safety, and clarity with everything and everyone on the spiritual plane is our birthright. If you don't yet know this, please consider making space for the possibility that it's true.

My Experience With This

When I was learning to build my intuitive skills, the idea was often reinforced that there are beings on the spirit side who are more powerful than humans, who can confuse, possess, or manipulate us, and they're looking for opportunities to take advantage of that. These beings were labeled evil, malicious, or negative. Having grown up in a religion that teaches that very concept, I heeded the advice to avoid them whenever possible, and when that wasn't possible, to interact with them as opponents in the battle between good and evil.

So I reached out to "positive" beings and quickly shut down any communications I encountered with "negative" beings. While doing that, I couldn't shake the fact that by the definitions of good and evil used to define non-physical beings, some of my own emotions and behaviors meant I was at times one of the evil ones. I knew those emotions and behaviors were my awkward expressions of the wounds I carried from experiences in this lifetime, and there was more to me than that.

In my emerging awareness of myself as a healer, I already knew that I'm here to help those who are out of balance, not to avoid them. That persistent whisper eventually encouraged me to set aside the fear and aversion I'd been taught about those who demonstrate "evil" behaviors, including myself. I began inviting contact with all beings on the spirit plane and I quickly learned there is no such thing as evil.

Staying Grounded

To be effective on the physical plane, you need to understand the insights you receive, be able to explain them to others, and understand how they apply to life. Grounding will help you do this. Even if you're naturally very grounded, it's helpful to intentionally ground yourself after you've been interacting through your intuition.

Some easy ways to ground yourself:

♥ Drink a large glass of water.
♥ Carry a grounding stone in your pocket or hold one in your hand. Good grounding stones include ordinary pebbles or gravel, black tourmaline, smokey quartz, and hematite.
♥ Touch your bare hands or feet to the earth, a rock, or a pot of soil.

Expanding Your Own Being

The biggest challenge you may face to maintaining full intuitive and spiritual awareness is choosing to stay awake in the presence of repeated reminders of imbalances in the world. This awareness can quickly become overwhelming if you think it's your responsibility to act on a lot of it or if you don't give yourself enough downtime. Remember, there's only so much you can do at any one time and during any one lifetime. Be kind to yourself about this.

If you find yourself overwhelmed by your awareness, a simple way to handle this is to gently expand your aura until it's bigger than any challenge you could ever face. Quietly stay in that expanded energy for a few minutes before going on about your day.

Some signs that you're overwhelmed by your awareness:
- ♥ Chronic exhaustion, angst, or anxiety
- ♥ A sense that you'll never have enough time
- ♥ Revulsion or disgust with humanity or the physical plane
- ♥ Desire to isolate for the long term
- ♥ Desire to stop knowing – to shut down your awareness

Choosing Down Time

As your intuitive skills develop you'll tend to notice layers of other people's lives that aren't yours to examine. This can be especially prominent in close relationships. Be kind to yourself and the people around you by giving yourself permission to be "off duty" when you're not intentionally working and when you're with people who haven't asked you to facilitate healing or provide insight.

One way to help yourself do this is to remind yourself that your intuitive awareness is yours to control. Being intuitively open is not the same thing as being at the mercy of a renegade sense. When you don't want to see something with your physical eyes, you either close them or you look elsewhere – you ignore what's available to be seen. Do the same with your spirit eyes and ears – it's ok to ignore what you feel or intuit from other people.

The Humor of Those in Spirit

There are some really funny things that happen during intuitive communications with some souls. Everyone, everywhere, loves to share some fun or a laugh from time to time. When something like this occurs, just laugh and thank your visitor for the fun.

Here's some of the spirit humor I've experienced...

A friend had recently died and I knew she'd visit at some point but hadn't heard from her yet. My partner and I were talking about this over breakfast one morning while all of our cats peacefully ate their breakfast on the other side of the kitchen. Suddenly and in perfect step with each other, all six cats arched their backs and carefully backed away from their food dishes. As soon as we laughed and greeted our friend by name, all six cats relaxed and went right back to eating. We'd never seen them do that before and we never saw it again.

Standing on the roof of my house installing a stainless steel chimney liner, I had easily connected each of the first four sections and slid them into the chimney. When I connected the fifth section the weight was suddenly at the limit of my physical strength. I was home alone, had three more sections to connect, couldn't continue to hold the weight much longer and couldn't get the sections that were already in the chimney to pull back out. After several minutes of frustrated attempts, concern for my safety, and more than a little sense of helplessness, I got angry. As I stood there clinging to the chimney liner so it wouldn't slide out of my reach and get stuck or damaged, I yelled at the goddess Diana. She was the strongest female archetype I could imagine in the moment and I definitely needed physical strength. I pretty plainly told her to prove to me that those in spirit are capable of making a tangible impact on the physical plane by helping me get that liner out of the chimney and get me and it safely to the ground. And there was no response other than my own awareness of how absurd that demand sounded and my steadily slipping grip on the liner. As I paused to try and figure out what to do next, I inadvertently pulled the liner a few inches out of the chimney. I pulled again and it kept coming. Fifteen minutes later I had myself and the whole liner safely on the ground and I felt a whisper of laughter in the air around me.

When I was first learning to initiate contact with spirit guides, a guide named Gray Smoke introduced herself to me. For a variety of reasons, I thought I had imagined the name. I talked with her anyway and then asked for proof that she was real. She told me to look out the back window of my house. I went to the window and saw gray smoke coming from the roof of my barn. Of course I thought the barn was on fire. I ran downstairs and met my partner in the kitchen. She'd also seen the smoke and was on her way to get me. We ran to the barn…no smoke, no fire, no smell, no damage. Went inside the barn, same thing. Walked all around the barn…no smoke, no fire, no smell, no damage. As we stood there wondering what had happened, I felt Gray Smoke quietly say, "told you so".

While driving home from a particularly fun evening with friends, I noticed a few street lights blink off when I got near them. Then I noticed a few more. Then I realized every street light I approached blinked off just before I got to it and blinked back on a few seconds after I passed by. This went on consistently for several blocks until I started laughing about the absurdity of it. From there on, the streetlights stayed on all the way to my house.

During a time when I believed special things had to happen to facilitate communication with those on the spirit side, I lit a candle each time I wanted to contact spirit. I carefully chose the candle color and holder, and lit the candle in a special way. After many months of doing this, one day the candle wouldn't light. The candle, wick, and matches were fine and there was no breeze. No matter what I did, that candle just wouldn't light. I decided to go ahead without it and soon heard my grandpa's laughter. No words, just his laughter. Grandpa didn't stand on formality about much of anything and I quickly made the connection that my candle was a bit of unnecessary formality.

CHAPTER 12
BECOMING INTUITIVELY FLUENT

To help you move beyond anything in life that's limited your access to your intuition, you'll find some specific skill building activities later in this chapter. In addition to those specific activities, frequently playing with activities like the ones listed below will help you reclaim your innate intuitive awareness. My suggestion is that you randomly choose and do one or more of these each day for at least 6 – 8 weeks. An intuitive way to play with these could be to open the book to this list, close your eyes and lay your finger somewhere on the page. Then do whatever activity your finger is pointing at.

♥ Question the facts. Periodically listen to an expert on a subject and wonder what they've left out of the conversation. Focus on one thing that's said and give your mind permission to imagine why that matters, how it was figured out, and if it's the only accurate perspective.

♥ Push your limits. Do something you believe is beyond your ability.

♥ Do it backwards. Choose something simple, like walking up the stairs, and do it backwards.

♥ Accept someone else's truth as "also true". Take in the perspective of someone you disagree with about a topic you understand well. Explore ways that both of your perspectives could be equally true.

♥ Transform dissonance into resonance. Arrange scraps of various colors of fabric or paper into patterns that look conflicted to you. Then add some pieces between the conflicted ones, creating a transition that changes each conflict into a harmonious flow.

♥ Close your eyes and sit quietly for a few seconds. Then, with your mind, feel into the space behind you and imagine what's there. Open your eyes and look at what's really there.

♥ Sitting quietly by yourself, focus on what you think will occur one hour from now in the immediate environment you'll be in at that time. Write it down in as much detail as you can. In one hour, compare what you wrote with what's actually occurring.

♥ Watch something that's going on around you and imagine how the situation will develop over the next few minutes. Continue watching and see if your imagined scenario resembles what actually develops.

♥ Focusing on a recent experience that you shared with someone else, imagine how that other person saw you in the experience. Write down what you get and then ask the other person if this is true.

♥ Choose a project that you know how to do and before starting it, imagine a different way to do it. Do the project in the way you imagined and see how it turns out.

♥ Using no instructions, do something you don't know how to do. Choose something relatively simple the first few times you do this. Consider what you want to accomplish, break it down into steps, and try doing a step the way you think it can work. If it doesn't work, pause and then try the same step a different way that you think will work. Keep going until you get it figured out.

♥ Strengthen your confidence in your relationship with Spirit, your spirit guides, and your spirit animals by inviting them to hang out with you for a few hours. Pay attention to your awareness of them during that time.

♥ Allow yourself to wonder if seemingly random things have a connection to each other or a message for you. Many things just are what they are so don't try to make something mean anything other than what's obvious. Just allow for the possibility that there's more to it than meets the eye. An easy way to do this is to focus your attention on something and ask, "If this is connected to that, what might the connection be?" or "If there's a message here for me, what might it be?"

Helpful Basics

Let intuitive awareness be normal

Allowing your intuition to be consciously present during normal daily activities will develop your ability to access this as desired. As you're going about your normal activities allow yourself to notice unrelated thoughts that show up and take a few seconds to see where they lead you. Don't let this become something that interrupts what you're doing, just let it be something you notice along with what you're doing.

If your normal thinking is primarily logical

Your most likely challenge will be trusting thoughts that appear to be random, imaginary, or just don't make sense to you. A good way to begin working with this is to notice those types of thoughts with a bit of curiosity and entertain the possibility that they may be real.

If your normal thinking is primarily creative

Your most likely challenge will be noticing the difference between your thoughts that are solidly connected with life on the physical plane and your thoughts that are not. A good way to begin working with this is to focus on your body (not your mind) and notice if your body feels a solid connection with the thought. If it does, the thought is well connected with life on the physical plane.

Sensory sensitivities

Particularly while you're getting accustomed to being intuitively open, you may become less comfortable in situations that include a lot of sensory stimulation. Discomfort with crowds, bright lighting, and a lot of noise are the situations I hear the most about. This is sensory overload and it happens because you're not yet accustomed to being aware with all of your senses.

Please remember, you get to choose what you respond to. It's ok to ignore the things you don't want or need to be aware of. It's ok to avoid high stimulation environments for awhile. It's also ok to ignore your intuition when you want to.

My Experience With This:

I've always been a bit sensitive to light and noise and this became more pronounced during my first couple of years with this work. I don't like being restricted by anything, including my own body, so I focused on learning how to be everywhere I want to be and still be intuitively open. For awhile, I spent less time in optional high stimulation environments like stores, parties, clubs, etc. When I had to be in high stimulation environments I made a point of stepping outside or pausing in calmer areas for a few minutes when I felt the need. This way of letting myself gently acclimate worked very well for me.

Grounding yourself

Intuitive insights are the most beneficial when you understand how they apply to ordinary life. Grounding yourself provides you with a reference point that connects your intuitive insights to the reality of life on Earth.

Some signs that you're not well-grounded:
- ♥ Confusion, forgetfulness, or scattered thinking
- ♥ Physical clumsiness or frequent accidents
- ♥ Lack of awareness of your physical surroundings

Some easy ways to ground yourself:
- ♥ Drink a large glass of water.
- ♥ Carry a grounding stone in your pocket, wear one in a piece of jewelry, hold one in your hand… Good grounding stones are ordinary pebbles or gravel, hematite, black tourmaline, and smoky quartz.
- ♥ Do something physical that requires your full attention.
- ♥ Do something that requires logical thinking.

♥ Eat a root food - this is any food with an edible part that grows underground.
♥ Put your bare hands or feet on the floor, earth, a rock, or a pot of soil and take a deep breath.

Developing focus

Most of us already know how to focus on things we're interested in. We know how to notice and ignore extraneous things and keep our focus where we want it to be. Connecting that existing skill set to your intuition is all that's needed.

Until this becomes natural for you, here's a way to expand your intuitive focus:
1. Set aside time to focus on receiving and understanding intuitive insights. Even 10 minutes on a regular basis will be beneficial.
2. Before starting these dedicated times, take care of anything that's likely to distract your attention.
3. If you have a time limit, set a timer so you don't have to watch the clock.
4. Give yourself permission to stay focused.
5. If interruptions or distractions occur, take them in stride, address them if needed, and then return to your focus.
6. Focus for slightly longer time periods each time you do this.
7. If you get bored, stop.

Choosing how and what you want to notice

The purpose of intuitive interactions and connections with souls on the spirit side is to have a beneficial impact on everyone involved. While you're learning to be intuitively wide awake you'll probably experience inconvenient timing, awkward contacts, and unwanted information. If this unsettles you, give yourself permission to connect gently and respectfully with all beings, spiritual and physical. Support yourself in that by telling Spirit that you'll only respond to invitations from the spirit plane that are gentle and respectful.

Just like sights, sounds, smells, and activities in your physical environment, the things you notice intuitively aren't always under your control. Who and what you respond to and how you respond are always under your control. If you don't want to notice certain types of intuitive information or spiritual contact, ignore them. If you want to experience more, focus on them.

Intuitive information comes from these sources:
♥ Our own higher self, soul, creative thinking, or lived experience.
♥ Beings other than ourselves – this can be living people, those in spirit, plants, animals, etc.
♥ Spirit – the being or energetic force that's the combination of all. I call this

"All That Is and All That Is Not". Some people use the name God, Allah, The Great Mystery, Creator, The Timeless One, etc.

Intuitive information arrives in these ways:
- ♥ Spontaneously while dreaming or while engaged in wide awake conscious experiences or thoughts.
- ♥ During dedicated times while doing activities such as meditation, trance, semi-trance, readings, healing sessions, etc.

It arrives in these forms:
- ♥ Thoughts, mentally or physically spoken words, reading, writing
- ♥ Mental or physical pictures, colors, images, or objects
- ♥ Physical touch or activity
- ♥ Sounds, melodies, scents

My Experience With This
I receive most of my intuitive interactions while I'm wide awake and fully conscious. Sometimes this is during meditation; most of the time it's during my normal daily activities. The rest of my interactions occur during my sleeping dreamtime. Every now and again a soul contacts me in an awkward way. When this happens, I continue interacting with them kindly while they figure out how to interact with me kindly.

When I'm awake thoughts come to me, sometimes one word at a time, sometimes in full sentences. When I don't fully understand the words, sometimes I receive mental images that help clarify the message. These conversations almost always begin with one word or thought that's out of context for what I'd been thinking, or that I sense isn't my own. When I notice that, I pause to see what comes next. If more comes, I begin interacting with whoever is speaking to me, whether or not they identify themselves.

When I'm asleep, sometimes I wake up slightly in the midst of intuitive interactions. Sometimes I sleep all the way through and become aware of them when I wake up in the morning.

Awake or asleep, I tend to experience these sensations, thoughts, and emotions:
- ♥ Light pressure, warmth, or coolness
- ♥ A feel that someone else is nearby when no one is physically there
- ♥ A light touch on the back of my neck
- ♥ A hand touching or holding mine
- ♥ Chills up or down my spine

♥ One eye feels focused on one direction and the other eye feels focused on a different direction

♥ Thoughts have entered my head from just behind my right ear

♥ "What's that?"… like something just passed by my peripheral vision and I didn't quite catch what it was.

♥ "Hmm, I wonder if that's true?"… like I've just been invited to explore something that's not quite solid.

♥ "That's what I've been looking for."… like a puzzle piece just fell into place.

♥ Calm, kindness, love

Accurately understanding your insights

Knowing how to set aside the filters of your own perspectives, expectations, and beliefs is an essential part of accurately understanding intuitive information. Intuitive insights can reach into areas that are beyond previous experience or proven knowledge and because of this, the information you receive will often be unprovable until after it's been delivered or acted on. The idea that you'll be certain it's accurate when you deliver it is one of the first expectations you'll need to set aside.

If you're someone who likes to know you're "right" before you speak, you'll benefit from choosing to be comfortable with "wrong" sometimes. If you're someone who likes to say whatever comes to your mind, you'll benefit from choosing to pause and feel for accuracy before you speak.

Sometimes you'll receive insights that truly feel accurate to you and that inspire the recipient to act, even if the details of the message don't make sense or turn out to be inaccurate. This tends to occur when the recipient needs a push to move beyond something that's undermining their well-being. The benefits of this type of insight are usually obvious shortly after the person acts on them. The feel you'll have with this type of insight is just the same as an accurate insight. You'll feel its accuracy and unless you're the recipient, you'll have no attachment or urgency about the recipient acting on it.

Here are some simple ways to expand your intuitive accuracy:

♥ Start with simple, insignificant insights first. Then expand the complexity and importance as you gain confidence.

♥ Write your insight down and give yourself time to see if things play out that way in real life.

♥ Act on your insight and see what happens.

♥ Ask another person if your insight resonates with them or if it makes sense to them.

♥ Ask spirit if your interpretation is true and notice how your body responds to that. If your body tenses up, you're interpreting through a filter. If your body relaxes, you're on track.

Skill Building Techniques

While you're learning, please explore as many of the following activities as feel right to you at any given time. If you're aware of other activities that help develop intuitive skills, play with them too. Receiving intuitive information can open your mind to things that fascinate you and to things you never thought about before. Let this be a fun adventure!

I've included basic information about how to do the techniques listed in this section; there are also many other resources available for learning how to use these techniques and others. You can find books and courses online and there may be teachers in your local community. I encourage you to learn from at least a few different books and/or teachers for each tool you decide to use.

My suggestion is that you set aside times to focus specifically on each method that interests you. Be patient with your learning process. It's normal to do most of these things quite a few times before getting information that makes sense or insights that are accurate. Some techniques are more complex than others and take more time to learn fluently. Some tools and techniques will work better for you than others. If you quickly get accurate, complex insights using a specific technique, you'll probably find it helpful to use that as a primary way to continue developing your intuitive skills.

Automatic Writing

This is a way of consciously channeling intuitive information. During the first few months that you're learning this technique it's helpful to have a set time, day and location to do this. This helps your mind get into a routine, which makes the learning process more efficient. One hour at a time, once a week for three or four months is beneficial.

You'll need:
♥ A notebook or pad of paper. A spiral bound notebook works great by allowing you to write on both sides of each page without having to open your eyes when you need a fresh page.
♥ Something to write with. Use a pencil if you're concerned about leaving marks on things if you run off the edge of the page.

Place the notebook sideways on your writing surface so you can write across the long side of the pages and hold your pen or pencil in the hand you normally write with. Close your eyes and keep them closed until you're done writing.

1. Begin by breathing gently and bringing yourself to center.
2. Starting in the upper left corner of the page, begin moving your pen or pencil in scrolling loops without trying to write specific letters or words. If your native language is read from right to left, start in the upper right corner of the page. Be patient with this – during your first several sessions it's normal to get a lot of meaningless loops and scribbles. Don't be concerned about legibility – that will develop with time.
3. When you get to the edge of the paper, move down the page a bit and keep writing. Don't worry about line spacing – that will develop with time.
4. When you get to the end of the page, flip it over and keep writing.
5. Keep writing for at least thirty minutes each time you do this. Again, be patient, it may take four or more sessions to get legible words and longer to get legible sentences.
6. When you're done writing for the day, open your eyes and look carefully at what's on the pages. When you start getting legible words, it's normal for them to be strung together without spaces between them. As you find them, putting a / mark at the end of each word will help with readability. If you're especially drawn to random words, highlight them in some way then go back and read them from the beginning of that day's writing to the end and see if all of them together make any complete sentences.
7. End the session by thanking whoever may have communicated with you during that session. Do this even if you don't know they were there or you were unable to write their messages.

My Experience With This

I used Automatic Writing as a learning tool. It helped me develop my ability to channel information from the spirit plane into words I can understand. It also helped me learn how to "be of two minds" at the same time – fully alert and present to my physical environment while consciously receiving information from those on the spirit plane. Among the adventures I had while writing this way, I developed solid relationships with some of my spirit guides and had my first clear communications with my deceased loved ones.

Conversations with Those in Spirit

Engaging in conversations with those in spirit is natural for us during our first few years of life here. Many of us forget how to do this or are taught to see these as imaginary conversations. Remembering how to have these conversations will help you initiate and engage in interactive relationships with any beings who live on the spirit plane.

Activities to build your communication with those in spirit

♥ Talk to deceased loved ones. The easiest way to begin doing this is to sit quietly, breathe gently and bring yourself to center. Then invite your loved one to join you. Pause silently for a few seconds before beginning to speak out loud to that person. While you're talking, tell them whatever is in your heart or mind. When you're done, sit quietly for about fifteen minutes and just receive whatever comes back to you. You may get words, emotions, sensations, scents, knowings, etc.

♥ Walk through a graveyard and gently feel the echoes and stories of those buried there. Pause at various graves and gently feel for the echoes and stories of that person or of people who loved them. If nothing comes to you at a specific grave, move on to a different one and pause there.

♥ Go to a museum and pause with objects that interest you. Gently feel into the space between you and the object for the echoes and stories of the object or any people who touched it.

♥ Walk slowly through old buildings or old parts of town and gently feel for the echoes and stories of events that occurred there.

My Experience With This:

Since learning to have this kind of communication, my conversations with those in spirit have always flowed back and forth easily. They typically turn into conversations that are several minutes long and include a lot of appreciation and love for each other, even if we've never met in any other way.

When I initiate a personal conversation with a soul, I often begin by speaking out loud directly to whoever I want to talk with. Sometimes I continue my side of the conversation out loud, most of the time I shift to thought speaking as soon as they respond to me. When a soul initiates contact with me, I tend to feel their presence for a second, then thoughts start coming to me. I respond with thought speaking, and sometimes by speaking verbally. I usually don't hear their words spoken out loud.

Divination Tools

It's helpful to use a divination tool to build your skills at receiving and interpreting intuitive messages. After those basic skills are built, a lot of healers continue to use these tools with clients as well as for their own spiritual and personal development. If you enjoy certain tools, keep using them as long as that feels right to you.

Some of the most commonly used divination tools are Tarot Cards or other types of divination cards, Runes, Tea Leaves, Pendulums, Astrological Charts, and Dowsing Rods. Here are a few of my favorites:

♥ Dowsing Rods – these are usually thin L shaped copper rods, or flexible Y shaped tree branches. They're used to detect energy, emotions, minerals, water, and a variety of other things. Basically, you lightly hold a copper rod in each hand, or an upper section of the Y shaped branch in each hand. Then you center yourself, focus on what you're trying to discover, and let the dowsing rods move however they move.

♥ Pendulum – this is usually a stone or pendant hanging from a chain or string. Basically, you hold the free end of the chain or string gently between your thumb and forefinger in a way that allows the stone or pendant to swing freely. Center yourself, then keeping your arm and hand very still, ask the pendulum to show you a "yes" and notice how it swings. Then ask it to show you a "no" and notice how it swings. When it stops swinging, continue holding your arm and hand still and ask a question that can be answered with "yes" or "no".

♥ Tarot Cards or other types of divination cards – these come in decks with various numbers of cards. Basically, you focus on a question or situation, shuffle the cards and pull some of them, then lay them in a formation and interpret the story they tell you.

Some ways to increase your accuracy with divination tools:
♥ Do a lot of readings for yourself and others.
♥ When reading for others, ask them for feedback about your accuracy.
♥ After reading for yourself, make a point of noticing which information from the reading proves to be true and which doesn't.

Meditation

Meditation is the practice of stilling your mind and becoming fully present to the current moment. It helps develop intuitive skills by supporting your abilities to focus and to notice subtle things within you and around you. Some people meditate by sitting or lying still. Some by dancing, walking, or running, and some meditate by doing ordinary activities that don't require their full attention.

While meditating, some people focus on their breath or a stationery object until that becomes all they notice, allowing the rest of their mind to rest or wander. Some focus on a specific topic or question and, coming from the assumption that all they notice or think during the meditation relates to that focus, they allow their mind to wander.

There are specific meditation techniques you can learn. You can also create your own by playing with a variety of activities that calm your mind while maintaining your mental clarity. I don't recommend using mind-altering substances during meditation – even small amounts reduce your conscious thinking to a level that's counterproductive for meditation.

Psychometry

This is a way of receiving insights by holding or touching an object. When doing a reading for someone, it's helpful if the object is one they cherish or one they use or wear frequently.

While you're learning, it's helpful to do this type of readings for people you're comfortable with. It's also helpful to check your accuracy several times while you're reading the object. An easy way to do this is to share some information you've received and then ask the person if it's accurate, makes sense to them, or resonates with them. This will help you see if you're clearly receiving what's really there, interpreting insights through your own filters, or catching only parts of the message.

To read this way:
Begin by holding the object gently in the palm of your hand, closing your eyes and bringing yourself to center. Then pay attention to any thoughts or sensations that come to you. The longer you hold the object, the more clearly and deeply you'll read its energy so stay with this for several minutes.

While you're noticing what's coming to you from the object, it's fine to open your eyes and look at the object, move it around in your hand, keep your eyes closed the whole time, or go back and forth between open and closed eyes. If at any time you want to speak out loud about what you're noticing, do so.

Soul Overlays

This helps open the part of your mind that remembers other lifetimes and times between lives. Sometimes when doing this, you'll remember specific experiences of your other ways of being. If you don't have any memories while doing this, just enjoy the ability to see some of the shifts in appearance you've made when you've moved from one way of being to another.

In a room with low light, or no light, stand or sit in front of a mirror. Put a lit candle or flashlight, shining up toward the ceiling, about 8" out from your body and about 4" – 10" below your chin. Focus on your face in the mirror and soften your eyes a bit. Without moving your facial muscles, continue looking at your face until you see subtle changes in it. You may see continual changes or a couple of variations that appear and linger. What you're seeing are overlays of your own faces from other ways of being.

My Experience With This

The first time I did this, it took a few minutes before I noticed any changes to my face. After the energy started flowing, I saw constant changes for about ten minutes. I was really fascinated so I continued to do this frequently for several months, each time seeing different versions of myself. The changes I saw sometimes looked like shadows moving across part of my face and sometimes like semi-transparent faces sitting in front of my face. When I focused on them, they'd often expand to cover my whole face, head, and neck. Sometimes the shifts were subtle, sometimes my entire appearance changed radically.

Perceiving Auras & Body Energies

We're capable of being aware of body energies and auras in and around all living physical beings. Although the energy patterns differ somewhat between species, all contain colors we can either physically see or intuitively discern when we understand what we're seeing or perceiving.

Human energy is visible around the entire body, and the colors tend to be brighter and more substantial around the head and shoulders. A typical human aura has a narrow dark band just outside the physical body and a narrow bright band just outside of the dark band. Outside of the bright band there's a collection of various colors that may be solid or semi-transparent.

The colors, energy patterns, and transparency vary from person to person and vary based on the person's current emotions, health, and thoughts. These colors often cover large areas. They're dynamic energies so they tend to shift shape and depth of color in a pretty steady flow. Watching or feeling them is a bit like watching the northern lights.

Physical body energy and aura energy can feel warm, hot, cool, or cold. It can feel dense, light, heavy, sticky, gentle, harsh, porous, or spongy.

Energy that's balanced tends to have colors that are bright, vibrant, or soft and may feel welcoming, comfortable, understandable, or gentle. Energy that's out of balance tends to have colors that are a bit dull, muddy, or murky and may feel confusing, uncomfortable, harsh, or closed. The temperature and consistency of energy is often discernible when you gently hold the palm of your hand on or over the area for a minute or two.

Seeing energies with your physical eyes

The easiest way to help your eyes remember how to physically see these energies is to begin by playing with this with another person and focus on their aura to start with. When you're comfortable seeing someone's aura, look for energies within their body.

Seeing auras is easiest if you begin learning in a room with a wall area that's blank and is a neutral color – soft gray, off-white, or light tan work very well. Dim the lighting without making it dark. With the person standing or sitting in front of the wall, focus your eyes on their throat or face and then soften your eyes. Without moving your eyes, notice what you see around the edges of their head and shoulders. Then shift your focus to another area of their body, soften your eyes again and notice what you see around the edges of their body.

Seeing energies within the body is done the same way, but it's not necessary to have a neutral background or dim lighting. Ask the person to sit or lay still wherever you're both comfortable and, with your eyes softened, look at a specific area of their body. Keep looking for a few minutes and notice what you see in that area.

Perceiving energies with your hands

For most people, this is the easiest way to begin perceiving energies. To get a feel for how to use your hands this way, gently lay the palm of one of your hands on your own body. Your touch should be feather-light and feel nurturing and kind to you. Let your hand rest there for several minutes and notice the sensations, thoughts and emotions that come to you while doing this; see if they weave together into a message you understand. When you feel complete with that location on your body, move your hand to another place on your body and repeat the process.

Perceiving energies with your intuition

This is a process of mentally or physically noticing energies and their colors, consistency, and purpose. The easiest way to develop your ability to intuitively notice energies is to sometimes play with this on your own, and sometimes with another person who will give you feedback about what you perceive.

Here's a process for learning to see this way:

1. Hold your hands out in front of you about twelve inches, with your palms together and gently touching each other.
2. Relax your hands and rub your palms together in a circular motion for a minute or so until you feel some heat between them.
3. Move your palms an inch or so apart and bend your fingers a little so they form a roundish hollow between your palms.
4. Move your palms eight to ten inches apart and then slowly move them toward each other, noticing any sensations in your palms and fingertips as they get closer together.
5. Repeat this as needed until you can feel the energy without having to rub your palms together.
6. When you have a sense of how energy feels in the palms of your hands, hold one or both hands about 6" away from another person.
7. Keeping your hands about 6" away from the other person, with your palms facing them, slowly move your hands around their body, pausing in one spot for a bit as you're inspired to. Notice any sensations in your hands while you're doing this.

My Experience With This

Initially I found it easier to feel energy with the palms of my hands than to physically see it or to perceive it intuitively. The sensations I receive tend to be light pressure, warmth, coolness, or a feel of something gently flowing through my hands.

Receiving thoughts about where someone's energy needs attention developed from my ability to feel energy with my hands. When I receive thoughts this way, I tend to feel the thought enter my mind just behind my right ear. It feels like a gentle distraction at first – like something just popped in that doesn't quite belong. By following the thought, I find that the whole message unfolds in an understandable way.

Recognizing when I saw energy with my physical eyes came quite awhile after I was skilled at feeling and perceiving energies. At that point, I realized I'd been seeing auras for years and had thought something was wrong with my eyes.

I see energy with my physical eyes by focusing my vision on a center point and allowing the edges to soften to a slight blur. When I focus on a different center point, I do the same thing. By looking at the energy this way, I physically see aura colors as well as patterns and colors within physical bodies.

While looking at someone's face the same way, I physically see overlays of faces they wore in other lifetimes. For me these show up as semi-transparent images sitting slightly in front of the person's current face, or as changes in the appearance of the person's current face.

When I return to my normal visual focus, all of the colors, patterns, and facial overlays disappear.

SECTION 4

HEALING TECHNIQUES

I find paths to wholeness.

This section includes the specific techniques I use most often. Many of them can be made into full length sessions, although I seldom do that. I tend to include a variety of techniques in each session, flowing with what comes up for the client as we move through the session. Many of these techniques can be used with any being living on Earth. For those living in spirit, intuitive communication is typically all that's needed.

Please also use these techniques for your own growth and healing – many of them can easily be self-guided. When learning healing techniques I always work with them on myself first, then with friends or family until I get comfortable with the technique. When you're comfortable working with these techniques, please feel free to adapt them to your own ways of working with clients.

Some of these techniques can be done by clients on their own. Instructions for them to use on their own are in Section 6 – Self-Guided Healing Techniques.

CHAPTER 13
ACCESSING CORE WISDOM

Plan on about 20 minutes for this process. This is a guided meditation and it can only be done when the client actively participates.

While doing this your client needs to stay present to their own body so please don't physically touch them while in process. You'll make some requests and then let your client lead the way in identifying where the energy is in their own body and what they need to re-balance it.

Accessing Core Wisdom is used to heal beliefs and perceptions that keep people disempowered, questioning their own competence, dependent on others, unable to move beyond painful experiences, unable to grow beyond reactive defenses, etc. It's also used to help people regain access to their inborn wisdom and to skills they've forgotten or blocked due to family dynamics or life experiences.

To identify when this technique is useful listen for things your client holds to be true, natural, or universal that you know aren't. Here are some examples:
- You, or others you know of, respond differently than your client does to the same type of situation.
- Your client makes comments such as:
  - When someone yells like that your feelings get hurt.
  - Everyone gets angry when…
  - That's not good for anyone.
  - Of course I was sad when...

You may notice multiple beliefs or perspectives that need balancing. These will typically be supporting each other in some way and they can be worked with consecutively in this process. I prefer to work with no more than two or three of these in the same session.

Accessing Core Wisdom Process:
Throughout this process, make no suggestions about what your client's answer may be – this is completely about what comes from within them. Regardless of their answer, work with it. Even "I don't know" or "nothing comes" are workable answers for this healing process.

If your client has difficulty finding the places where their body wants healing, remind them to pay attention to their body's response, not to their mind. If needed, let them know their body may show them where to touch by feeling an itch, ache, tickle, warmth, coolness, tension, a desire to move, etc.

To help your client stay present to self rather than interacting with you, ask them to keep their eyes closed through this entire process.

Give your client the following instructions, one step at a time, pausing after each to give them the time they need:

1. Close your eyes and breathe gently, bringing yourself to center.
2. Now find the place in your body where you believe (…the perspective or belief that was identified) and gently lay your hand there when you find it.
3. I'm going to ask you a question and I want you to tell me the first thought that comes to your mind. It doesn't have to make sense so please don't over think it.
4. What do you need to bring this into perfect balance and harmony?
5. Now, bring (…the thought your client named exactly as they said it) down through your crown chakra at the top of your head and down through the center of your body to the place where your hand is. Fill that place with (…the thought they named exactly as they said it) until it's overflowing. Please tell me when that feels complete.
   - While your client does this, pay close attention to their energy and your intuition to see if anything else is ready to be re-balanced.
6. Now relax your hand back into your lap and take a slow deep breath.
   - If you feel it's needed, repeat the above steps for other beliefs or perspectives that you noticed are ready to re-balance. When your client is complete with this part of the process, go on to the next steps.
7. Now find the place in your body where you already know how to live every moment of your life with grace and with wisdom. Please gently lay your hand there when you find it.
8. I'm going to ask you a question and I want you to tell me the first thought that comes to your mind. It doesn't have to make any sense so please don't over think it.
9. What color do you find there?
10. Now bring (…the color your client named) down through your crown chakra at the top of your head and down through the center of your body to the place where your hand is.
11. Fill that place with (…the color your client named) until it's overflowing and tell me when that feels complete.
12. Now spread (…the color they named) through your entire body until every cell is saturated and then spread it out into your aura, in all directions including above and below, just as far as you can. Please tell me when that feels complete.
13. Whenever you're ready, open your eyes and tell me how you're feeling.

Please Let Your Client Know:

After receiving this type of healing, it takes about 48 hours for the energy to completely settle. Soaking for 20 minutes in a warm bath with lemon oil or juice, rosemary oil, or cedar oil added to the water will help their energy settle more quickly and gently.

During these 48 hours their emotions may be all over the place and that's ok. Ask them to not make decisions or relate to anyone based on their emotions during this time period. They need to just notice what they're feeling and let it be. Their emotions will settle by the time 48 hours have passed.

Within a few days they'll start noticing some shifts in their ways of being and the healing will continue to gently and naturally unfold for the next several days.

My Experience With This:

When I'm doing this type of work with somebody, I watch them intensely with both my physical eyes and my intuition. I'm looking for images or impressions of other lifetimes, shifts in their aura or body energy, and changes in their body language or facial expressions. All of those things help me understand their progress through this healing and any additional support they may need to fully integrate their expanded access to their own wisdom.

Here's how I notice the energetic changes:

Impressions from other lifetimes – thoughts that come to me or changes in the appearance of the person's face or body.

Shifts in aura or body energy – changes in the colors, shadows, patterns, or the quantity of energy around the person's body.

One of My Favorite Stories About Accessing Core Wisdom

During a session with a client who was embarking on a new business venture, I noticed he got impatient every time he talked about one aspect of the business. Even though he felt he needed to offer it for the benefit of his customers, he wasn't sure it would be profitable or that he'd even like doing it. A couple of months after doing this healing work, he found a very enjoyable and profitable way to give his customers the benefit he wanted them to have.

CHAPTER 14
ANCESTRAL LINEAGE HEALING

Plan on about 30 minutes for this process. This is a guided meditation process and it can only be done when the client actively participates. This can be done with one person or with two or more living relatives, and with biological or adoptive families.

Ancestral Lineage Healing is used to heal detrimental family dynamics that have come down through generations. This includes things such as inherited physical challenges, addiction, violence, detrimental cultural or religious heritage, abuse of any variety (including self-abuse)... It also includes detrimental emotional dynamics such as depression, arrogance, pessimism, rage, unworthiness, shame, judgmentalism... Regardless of the type of family dynamic you're working with, support your client in moving through this process with loving kindness for everyone involved. In addition to being a healing, this is a loving celebration of family wholeness.

It doesn't matter whether or not your client knows the names of their ancestors or anything about them – you'll be working with them based on their kinship to the client not their identity during their lifetime.

Regardless of the number of challenges within a family, focus exclusively on one dynamic per session and wait at least one week between sessions. This healing unfolds gently for many months as it ripples through the family and often one session will heal multiple dynamics.

Ancestral Lineage Healing Process:
Begin by talking with your client about the family dynamic they want to focus on until both of you can name it clearly and succinctly, ie: addiction, poverty, etc. When you're both clear about the focus you're ready to begin.

To help your client stay present to self rather than interacting with you, ask them to close their eyes and keep them closed through this entire process.

Here's how I feel the ancestors gathered when beginning this healing process:

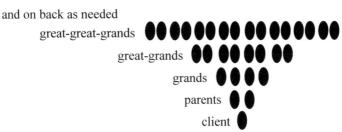

Give your client the following instructions, one step at a time, pausing after each to give them the time they need:

1. Close your eyes and breathe gently, bringing yourself to center.

2. Call in your parents, asking your father to stand behind one shoulder and your mother behind the other. Please tell me when you feel them here.

3. Call in all four of your grandparents, asking them to stand behind their child, starting to form a V that goes back and outward, expanding toward the left and right. Please tell me when you feel them here.

4. Call in all eight of your great-grandparents, asking them to stand behind their child, expanding the V back and outward to the left and right. Please tell me when you feel them here.

5. Call in all sixteen of your great-great-grandparents, asking them to stand behind their child, expanding the V back and outward to the left and right. Please tell me when you feel them here.

6. Now call in all of your grandparents from there as far back in time as they're willing to respond, asking each of them to stand behind their child, expanding the V back and outward to the left and right. Please tell me when that feels complete.

7. Ask your ancestor who first introduced (…name the detrimental dynamic) into the family to light up in some way so everyone knows who this person is. Please tell me when that feels complete.

8. All of you together, turn and face this loved one and send her/him love and healing until this person indicates the healing is complete. Please tell me when that feels complete.

9. Call in all of your aunts, uncles, and cousins from the oldest generations forward, up to but not including your generation. Please tell me when you feel them here.

10. Ask all of your direct ancestors to join you in spreading the healing sideways to all of your aunts, uncles, and cousins, beginning with the furthest back and moving forward up to, but not including your generation. Please tell me when that feels complete.

11. Call in all of your siblings and cousins in your own generation. Please tell me when you feel them here.

12. Now ask all of the generations before yours to spread the healing to your entire generation of the family, including you. Please tell me when this feels complete.

13. Now ask all who are gathered to turn and look to the future and join you in spreading the healing to all the children and grandchildren of your

generation and all generations as far into the future as you can reach. Please tell me when this feels complete.

14. Ask all who are gathered, including the future generations, to stand in a circle with you. When everyone is circled, step into the center of the circle and receive their love and gratitude for you being the one who initiated this healing. Stay with this until you feel overflowing with their love and gratitude. Please tell me when you feel full.

15. Return to your place in the circle and stand with your family as equals. Thank all of your relatives for participating and sit quietly as they each return to their own time and space.

16. Whenever you're ready, open your eyes and rejoin me here.

After your client opens their eyes, give them a few seconds then ask how they're feeling and help them gently ground.

Please Let Your Client Know:

After receiving this type of healing, it takes about 48 hours for the energy to completely settle. Soaking for 20 minutes in a warm bath with lemon oil or juice, rosemary oil, or cedar oil added to the water will help their energy settle more quickly and gently.

During these 48 hours their emotions may be all over the place and that's ok. Ask them to not make decisions or relate to anyone based on their emotions during this time period. They need to just notice what they're feeling and let it be. Their emotions will settle by the time 48 hours have passed.

Within a few weeks they'll start noticing some shifts in their ways of being and the healing will continue to gently and naturally unfold throughout their family for the next several years.

My Experience With This:

This is a level of experiencing family that steps beyond personalities and lifetime issues. For people whose families are deeply wounded, the potential pain of doing this may seem daunting. When a client is uncomfortable about doing this, I reassure them that this healing process is focused on healing, not on reviewing old wounds. If they're still uncomfortable I move on to something else.

The number of generations who show up to participate may range from two or three all the way into the hundreds. Some people are surprised by who participates and by the love and support they all share. I reassure clients that they're doing this right and there's more to their family than the pain they've known during this lifetime.

People are often unaware that a family challenge they've experienced actually began many generations back. It can take them a bit of time to focus on the one who introduced the challenge into the family rather than the one who introduced it to them. An approach I find helpful with this is to gently remind them to focus on the ancestor who is lit up. I don't ask them to not focus on the more recent person, I just remind them where I do want them to focus.

Some of My Favorite Stories About Ancestral Lineage Healing

A client came to me shortly after his dad died. His dad had been alcoholic and left behind a series of painful relationships with former wives, his own children, and several other people. Several younger members of the family had similar relationship patterns and were living with addictions. The man was very angry about the challenges his Dad had brought to the family and he wanted out of the family. By the end of this healing process he felt calm and had decided to stay connected with some of his relatives and see if things could change for the better.

When he contacted me again several years later, most of his relatives had grown beyond addictions. He knew he mattered to his family and was loved by them. He felt at peace about his Dad, had watched his mom heal from their difficult marriage, and felt that his family had finally learned how to love and be loved.

Ancestral Lineage Healing came to me in a dream. As with all techniques that I dream in, I work with them in my own life before offering them to others.

I began with my family's long-standing need to heal some religious dynamics that had become very divisive and painful. As I moved through the healing process, I found myself in the presence of hundreds of relatives spanning about twenty generations, all eager to heal this. I knew some of them; others I'd never heard of; others were yet to be born. I felt held and appreciated by my people at a depth I'd never before experienced, and that alone was very healing for me.

About three weeks after I did this healing work, some of my living relatives started talking with each other about these religious dynamics, which hadn't been openly discussed in decades. Over the course of the next few years most of my relatives who had continued to use these painful dynamics, softened about them and the rest of us felt them shift. Now, twenty years on, the role of religion in our family is gently shifting to include space for all of our spiritual paths.

CHAPTER 15
BODY PENDULUM

Plan on about 5 minutes for this process. This is a guided meditation process and it can only be done when the client actively participates.

Accessing truths and wisdoms this way can be helpful when stress is high or emotions are intense. It's also helpful when someone is having a difficult time making decisions.

This is best done with individual yes/no questions. If your client tends to include more than one question in a statement, have them separate those into individual questions and ask each one separately. A multiple question looks like this: Is it important for me to see my son tonight or can that wait until another time?

When doing this, "yes" means yes; "no" means no; "maybe" means the question isn't worded clearly or there are variables that make the answer uncertain.

Body Pendulum Process

Ask your client to sit or stand in a way that allows their body to sway slightly. Then give them the following instructions, one step at a time, pausing after each to give them the time they need:

1. Gently lay your hand on your solar plexus chakra and keep your focus there.
2. Now take a deep gentle breath and ask your body to show you a "yes". Pay attention to your body's response.
3. Now take a deep gentle breath and ask your body to show you a "no". Pay attention to your body's response.
4. Now take a deep gentle breath and ask your body to show you a "maybe". Pay attention to your body's response.
5. Now take a gentle deep breath, ask a clear yes or no question and pay attention to your body's response.

CHAPTER 16
BODY/MIND ALIGNMENT

Movement that symbolizes the change we want to grow into gets our physical being immediately involved in the process of bringing that change alive. This type of body experience is particularly helpful when a client's thinking is rigid, stuck, lacking confidence, resistant to the shift they want to make, or when they've never seen or experienced what they're trying to do.

This process is free flowing and creative. Basically, you'll come up with movements that fit your client's desired shift, then you'll invite your client to follow your instructions or to join you in doing it. Move with your inspirations as you're working with your client.

Here are some ideas:

♥ Becoming more flexible or creative:

Move spontaneously in any way that comes to mind. This tends to be difficult for people who have challenges being flexible or creative. In those situations, it can be helpful to begin with you leading and your client following your movements. Keep leading until you notice your client taking the lead and then follow their movements. When the time feels right, stop moving and acknowledge your client for taking the lead.

♥ Living into a specific outcome:

When you know what your client wants to achieve (good health, have a child, heal their marriage, change jobs, etc.), ask them to stand up and walk around until their body feels fully engaged. Then ask them to stay in that physical location and notice how it feels to be there. If they like the feel, ask them to continue walking until they feel complete.

If they don't like the feel, encourage them to rethink what they want to achieve – it may need to be shifted just a tiny bit, it may be something they really don't want but think they have to do. Then ask them to do the movement again.

~ or ~

Ask your client to state their intention as clearly as they can, then close their eyes and point in the direction where that possibility lives. Then ask them to open their eyes, walk to it, and stand in that location and absorb the energy.

~ or ~

If you have a large enough space or can work outdoors, ask your client to walk the path they think they'll need to take to manifest their intention. Then ask them to walk the path they want to take. If the two paths are different, discuss them until your client sees how the path they want to take will get them to the manifestation they want.

♥ Honoring personal boundaries:
   1. Ask your client to stand and face you. Hold your hands in front of you with your palms facing your client, at about shoulder height. Then ask your client to gently press their palms against yours.
   2. Now gently push your client's hands back toward them a bit, stepping closer to them while you're doing that. Stay there facing each other for a few seconds. The point here is to move into physical closeness that's not fully comfortable for your client.
   3. Now ask your client to push your hands back toward you a little, stepping closer to you while they're doing that. Stay there facing each other for a few seconds. The point here is for your client to push into your space to a point that's a little uncomfortable for them.
   4. Discuss how your client's body felt during each part of this. Those feelings are how their body tells them when they're honoring their own boundaries and the boundaries of another person.

♥ Engaging in a mutual, balanced relationship:
   1. Ask your client to stand and face you. Both of you hold your hands out with your palms facing each other, at about heart height.
   2. Touch your palms together lightly, holding contact and looking at each other for a few seconds. Then lean into each other's hands at the point midway between you. Then ask your client to lean in closer to you and pause there. Then you lean in closer to your client.
   3. The light touch at the midpoint between the two of you is the feel of a mutual relationship. The others are the feel of relationships where one partner is dependent on the other in some way.
   4. Discuss the experiences your client had regarding how their body felt and their emotions and thoughts in each position.

♥ Building self-trust
   Ask your client to keep their eyes closed, then ask them to stand up and slowly walk around while letting their feet tell them where to step next.
   - or -
   Ask your client to keep their eyes closed and dance with you.

One of My Favorite Stories About Body/Mind Alignment
My first experience with this was at a retreat with about twenty other people. I was asked to choose a goal I wanted to accomplish and thought would always

be out of my reach. After naming my goal, I was led to a wooded area that had some undergrowth and several dead trees lying on the ground. My task was to walk about eighty feet to the other side of the area, while keeping my eyes closed and staying focused on the goal I'd chosen. As I slowly walked, feeling my way with my feet, I found myself moving from uncertainty about achieving my chosen goal into the awareness that all goals are achieved by following our instincts about the next right step to take.

CHAPTER 17
EXPANDING SELF-TRUST

Plan on 3 to 5 minutes for this process. This is a guided meditation process and it can only be done when the client is actively participating.

This is used to ease panic or high stress and help your client calmly approach challenges they experience as overwhelming, intimidating, or dangerous. After doing this with a client I always encourage them to do this on their own any time they feel the need.

Expanding Self-Trust Process

Give your client the following instructions, one step at a time, pausing after each to give them the time they need:

1. Take a few gentle deep breaths and bring yourself to center.
2. Now focus on your solar-plexus chakra, breathe gently and imagine the color yellow filling that chakra.
3. Now gently expand the yellow through your entire body and out into your aura. Please tell me when this feels complete.
4. Now gently expand the yellow out as far as you can get it and then a little farther. Take it out so far that you're bigger than any challenge you could ever face. Please tell me when this feels complete.
5. Now pause in that expanded energy until you feel overflowing with it. Please tell me when this feels complete.
6. Now gently relax and allow the yellow to come all the way back into your solar-plexus chakra. Please tell me when this feels complete.
7. Whenever you're ready, open your eyes and rejoin me here.

Give your client a minute or two to resettle and then ask how they're feeling.

CHAPTER 18
CHAKRA BALANCING

Chakras are energy centers in our bodies and auras that support our ability to transform the energies around us into nourishment for our lives. All of us experience imbalances and blockages in our chakras from time to time. To keep ourselves thriving, it's beneficial to balance all of our chakras as a regular part of self-care. It's also beneficial to balance chakras after trauma, stress, extended travel, or illness. Books and online information and classes are readily available if you want to learn more.

The chakras listed below are the primary ones almost everyone depends on for well-being. The colors, musical notes and stones listed can be used to balance the chakra.

Primary Chakras

Root – located at the base of the tailbone. The primary function of this chakra is physical survival issues – food, shelter, & physical safety. The color is red and the musical notes are A and B flat (below middle C). Good stones to use for balancing are red jasper, red tiger-eye, garnet, ruby, hematite, red calcite.

When the root chakra is in balance your client will feel at ease with the well-being of their body. When it's out of balance they may experience some of the following: physical violence or the desire for it, overeating, undereating, constant hunger, frequent clumsiness, fear for their physical safety, little interest in sex or excessive interest in sex, light-headedness, inability to think clearly or stay focused, frequent exhaustion, frequent minor health problems, or lack of material necessities.

Belly – located about two inches below the navel. The primary function of this chakra is intimate connections with others – sexuality, childhood emotions, emotional intimacy, creativity, and family relationships. The color is orange and the musical note is B. Good stones to use for balancing are carnelian, citrine, realgar, brown tiger-eye, orange calcite.

When the belly chakra is in balance your client will feel high self-esteem, clear sexual energy, and easy flow in relationships. When it's out of balance, they may experience some of the following: fear, defensiveness, egotism, depression, addiction, self-defeating behavior, victimization, constipation, diarrhea, or problems in their reproductive organs.

Solar-Plexus – located in the soft spot below the breastbone where the ribs meet. The primary function of this chakra is personal power – the ability to be effective on the physical plane. The color is yellow and the musical notes are C and C sharp. Good stones to use for balancing are sulphur, amber, yellow zincite, yellow calcite, yellow topaz.

When the solar-plexus chakra is in balance your client will feel confident without being forceful. When it's out of balance, they may experience some of the following: self-righteousness, frustration, depression, anger, defeat, shyness, arrogance, egotism, ulcers, uncomfortable digestion.

Heart – located at the center of the breast bone. The primary function of this chakra is love – both self-love and love for others. The colors are green and pink and the musical notes are D and D sharp. Good stones to use for balancing are rose quartz, pink tourmaline, kunzite, rhodacrosite, watermelon tourmaline, malachite, emerald.

When the heart chakra is in balance your client will interact with herself/himself and others generously and with good will. She/he will feel loved and welcome and will give this to others. When this chakra is out of balance, they may experience some of the following: feeling isolated, unlovable, or unwilling to love, little or no compassion for self or others, a lot of solitude, shortness of breath, irregular heart rhythms.

Throat – located at the hollow at the base of the throat. The primary function of this chakra is communication – speaking personal truths, sharing information accurately and receiving information accurately. The color is blue and the musical note is E. Good stones to use for balancing are indicolite, lapis lazuli, turquoise, sapphire, sodalite.

When the throat chakra is in balance your client will speak their truth readily and clearly, communicate honestly in all interactions, identify and share their needs or desires in any situation, receive information accurately, and understand what others are saying. When this chakra is out of balance, they may experience some of the following: stay silent when they should speak up, misunderstand what others say, speak elusively or too forcefully, sore throat, laryngitis, other conditions that make it physically difficult to speak.

Third-Eye – located just above and between the eyebrows. The primary function of this chakra is the intellect – logical, creative, and intuitive. The color is purple and the musical note is F. Good stones to use for balancing are amethyst, sugulite, purple fluorite.

When the third-eye chakra is in balance your client will think clearly, follow logical and creative processes well, and be intuitively aware. When this chakra is out of balance, they may experience some of the following: mental illness, fuzzy thinking, short attention span, lack of intuition, blurred vision, tired eyes, headaches in the area of the chakra,

Crown – located at the top of the head – the spot that is soft on babies' heads. The primary function of this chakra is our connection with spirit. The colors are clear and gold and the musical notes are F sharp and G. Good stones to use for balancing are gold, clear quartz, diamond, herkimer diamond, yellow fluorite, yellow topaz.

When the crown chakra is in balance your client will be aware of the vastness of life, have a sense of their place in it, feel Spirit at work, and understand how to enact their own sacred work. When this chakra is out of balance, they may experience some of the following: boredom, futility, difficulty seeing from perspectives other than their own, rule bound, wandering in illusions, inability to bring their spiritual understanding into forms that are understandable to others, headaches, dizziness.

Palms of Hands – located in the center of each palm. The primary function of these two chakras is supporting hands-on healing and other forms of loving touch. The color is green and the musical note is D. Goods stones to use for balancing are emerald, flint, malachite.

When the palm chakras are in balance your client will readily and gently touch and receive touch. When these chakras are out of balance, your client may experience some of the following: lack of physical contact with others, isolation, depression, sore hands, unhealthy skin.

Soles of Feet – located in the center of each sole. The primary function of these two chakras is absorbing nourishment directly from the Earth and grounding in physical reality. The colors are brown and black and the musical resonance is drum beats. Good stones to use for balancing are fossils, petrified wood, apache tear, lava, pumice.

When the sole chakras are in balance your client will thrive. When these chakras are out of balance, your client may experience some of the following: lethargy, confusion about reality, dependence on others, muscular weakness, indigestion.

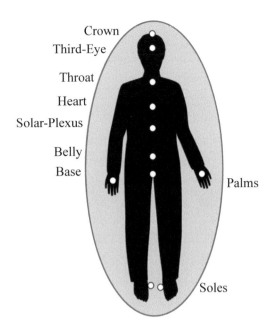

Crown
Third-Eye
Throat
Heart
Solar-Plexus
Belly
Base
Palms
Soles

Decreasing or Increasing Chakra Energy

This is done to support balance when someone is so focused on one aspect of life that other aspects are out of balance or neglected. This can be very beneficial during times of illness or high stress. When someone is out of balance this way, the energy of some chakras may need to decrease and others may need to increase.

Some indications this will be beneficial:
♥ Intense emotional expressions
♥ Frequent minor or major injuries
♥ Frequent clumsiness or forgetfulness
♥ Thought dominating emotion or emotion dominating thought
♥ Focus on living the aspects of one or more chakras while avoiding aspects of the other chakras

Process for Decreasing Chakra Energy

Gently lay the palms of both of your hands on the chakra for several minutes and focus on quieting and decreasing the energy flow within the chakra. Then lay a grounding stone on the chakra for five to ten minutes. Good grounding stones are: hematite, obsidian, smoky quartz, gravel

Process for Increasing Chakra Energy

Focus your attention on the chakra and take a few slow, deep breaths, allowing each breath to fill the chakra with vibrant energy. Take a few more slow, deep breaths, each time focusing on filling the chakra with its native color. Then, using a stone that's naturally the native color of the chakra, place it on the chakra and leave it there for five to ten minutes.

Ways to Balance Chakra Energy:

Do any one of these things…

♥ Smudge each chakra with sage.

♥ Lay a piece of kyanite on each chakra or have your client hold it in their hand with the striations running toward their finger tips.

♥ On each chakra, place a stone that you're intuitively drawn to or place a supportive stone for the chakra.

♥ Gently move your palms in a circular motion over each chakra, clockwise or counterclockwise, whichever direction intuitively feels right to you.

♥ Fill each chakra with its native color either by visualization or by laying an object of the appropriate color on the chakra.

♥ Play a drum at each chakra.

♥ Gently touch the tips of your thumbs and fingers to the tips of your client's toes and keep them there for a few minutes. Touch all fingers and toes at the same – your thumbs to your client's big toes, index fingers to second toes, middle to middle, ring to fourth, and little fingers to little toes.

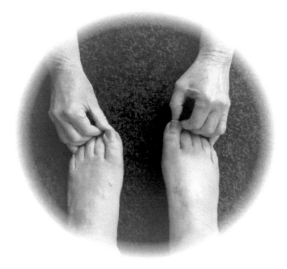

Reconnecting the Energy Between Chakras

This process is done to support a person's ability to fully align their actions with their intentions.

When a client repeatedly does any of the following, it's an indication this will be beneficial:

♥ Says one thing and does another
♥ Intends one thing and does another
♥ Lies, is in denial, or side-steps the truth in some other way
♥ Believes something and can't live it
♥ Dissociates
♥ Has trouble staying focused

Reconnection Process:

Lay a hand on each of the chosen chakras and imagine an arc of energy going up the front of the person's body from the lower chakra to the higher one, then through their body and down their back from the higher chakra to the lower one. Imagine the arc filling with the colors of both chakras until the colors blend together and move in a continuous circle. The work is complete when the circle of energy maintains itself.

CHAPTER 19
CORD RELEASE

Plan on about 10 minutes for this process. This is a guided meditation process and it can only be done when the client actively participates.

Cord Release is used to help people disengage from relationship dynamics that diminish their own well-being and from relationships that have ended. This is particularly beneficial with close family relationships and intimate relationships. Sometimes clients are concerned that doing this will end their connection to other person. It won't. What it will do is support your client in transforming the relationship into a healthy one by disengaging from the dynamics that are undermining it. When this is done for a relationship that has ended, it will help your client fully move on from that relationship and support their ability to embrace new relationships.

To identify when this technique is useful, listen for complaints, challenges, or grief your client repeatedly expresses about the same relationship. This will be a significant relationship that your client needs or wants to maintain, or feels they can't get out of. These relationships are usually family, romantic, close friendship, or professional.

Cord Release Process:
Give your client the following instructions, one step at a time, pausing after each to give them the time they need:
1. Close your eyes and breathe gently, bringing yourself to center.
2. Ask your (sister, mom, supervisor, ex…) to come join you and sit about six inches away facing you, mirroring your body posture without touching you.
3. Now take a slow deep breath and feel into the area between your bodies. You'll notice cords of two different colors there, running from your body to hers/his. The cords of one color belong to you and the other to her/him.
4. Now run your hand downward between your bodies, gently disconnecting her/his cords from your body and sliding them back over to her/him. If she/he tries to reconnect any of the cords, gently give them back again. Please tell me when that feels complete.
5. Now run your hand downward between your bodies again, and gently disconnect your cords from her/his body, bringing them back to you and laying them in your lap. Now let them gently dissolve into your body. Please tell me when that feels complete.
6. Now take a slow deep breath and again feel into the area between your bodies. Are there any more cords there?

- If your client finds additional cords, repeat steps 4, 5, and 6. When your client doesn't find any more cords, go to step 7.

7. Now thank her/him for being here and watch as she/he walks away and disappears completely.

8. Whenever you're ready, open your eyes and rejoin me here.

Give your client a minute or two to resettle and then ask how they're feeling.

CHAPTER 20
CRYSTALS & STONES

The simplicity of working with stones makes them very easy to include in any healing session. They work directly with the physical energy of the body in subtle ways that gently create lasting changes. I consistently find that when someone holds a stone or has a stone laying on or near them, they tend to stay grounded, fully present, and calm.

How Stones Work for Healing

When a particular stone aligns with a need, our body energy in that area naturally shifts to match the energy of the stone. As this shift occurs, the healing unfolds very gently – the most common experience is noticing the imbalances are no longer there. Books and online information and classes are readily available if you want to learn more. My favorite book on this topic is <u>Love Is In The Earth</u> by Melody.

Choosing the Stones

Basically, the right stones for you to use in your healing work are stones you're attracted to. The right stones for you to use with a client are the ones your client is attracted to or the ones you're drawn to during the session.

It's ok to go easy on your wallet while gathering your healing stones. The size and quality of a stone does nothing to enhance or diminish its ability to support healing. If you gather tiny pieces, putting them into a small pouch while you're working with them will help you keep track of them.

My own preference is stones in their natural form, and I do work with some that have been cut or tumbled. For me, the natural color of stones matters a lot in healing work so I avoid any that have been dyed or have been coated with something that changes their color or appearance.

Some stones, and some layouts, work particularly well with specific imbalances or types of growth. I've included some basic information about this later in the chapter and I highly recommend that you read a variety of books or articles about the healing properties of crystals and stones.

Some signs that a stone is aligned with how you intend to work with it:
♥ Your intuitive feel
♥ Visual attraction
♥ Feeling heat or cold from the stone
♥ Positive swing of a pendulum when it's held over the stone or you touch the stone.

Cleansing Crystals and Stones

There are many ways to cleanse crystals and stones that have been used in healing, have recently come into your care, or have been treated roughly in some way. The most important aspect of each of the methods is that it's done with the intention of giving the stone a rest so it can realign with itself.

I find it helpful to check intuitively from time to time and see if a stone's energy feels sluggish or clogged. If it does, I give it a rest until it feels clear again.

Some ways to cleanse crystals and stones
- ♥ Place the stone somewhere special to you and leave it there for however long feels right to you.
- ♥ Pass your hands over the stone with the intention its energy is realigning and refreshing.
- ♥ Set stones on a clear quartz cluster or a slab of selenite.
- ♥ Smudge stones with sage smoke.
- ♥ Wash stones in clear, cold water.
    Water will damage some stones and minerals – halite, apophyllite and azurite are some of them.
- ♥ Wash stones in salt water or bury them in sea salt for 24 hours
    Salt and salt water will damage some stones and minerals – hematite, opal, and pyrite are some of them.
- ♥ Set stones in direct sunlight for a few hours

Basic Healing Techniques
- ♥ Carry, wear, or sleep with the chosen stones for as long as feels appropriate.
- ♥ Put stones in your healing space and allow clients to hold or touch them.
- ♥ Have your client lie down for awhile within a layout of stones or arrange a layout on their body.
- ♥ Clear quartz points can amplify or reduce the energy of other stones.
    - To amplify: Lay a circle of quartz points around the stone(s), points directed toward it.
    - To reduce: lay a circle of quartz points around the stone(s), points directed away from it.
- ♥ When finished, seal the aura around your client's body by smoothing their aura with your hands.

Some of the Healing Stones

Amber
   ~ Grounding, supports decision making, draws out emotional pain, assists with assimilation of protein

Amethyst
   ~ Balances the third-eye chakra, anti-depressant, calms the mind, encourages transformation

Apophyllite
   ~ Enhances awareness during shamanic journey

Carnelian
   ~ Balances belly chakra, strengthens immune system, promotes emotional balance, increases physical energy, aids menstruation

Citrine
   ~ Balances belly chakra, clarifies differences between beliefs and feelings, aids relationships and digestion

Emerald
   ~ Balances heart chakra, aids meditation, overall healer

Flint
   ~ Supports ability to facilitate physical healing

Fluorite
   ~ Balances and integrates mental with physical, brain with body, and right side of brain with left side of brain

Kyanite
   ~ Balances all chakras

Lapis Lazuli
   ~ Balances throat chakra, aids clear communication, meditation, and expressions of kindness

Moonstone
   ~ Calming, aids meditation and intuition, balances lymphatic system

Onyx
   ~ Aids thinking, concentration, development of spiritual strength, practicality, grounding

Opal
   ~ Overall healer, aids ability to center, graceful physical movement, emotional detachment, and creativity

Pyrite
   ~ Balances solar-plexus chakra; amplifies and brings forth inner light, positivity, and creativity; aids allergy relief

Quartz

~ Clear – Balances all chakras, aids healing and meditation, magnifies energy

~ Blue – Aids calm healing of mental and emotional challenges, aids sleep

~ Rose – Balances heart chakra, comforts and calms, aids love for others and self-love

~ Smoky – Balances belly chakra, grounds, relieves depression and anxiety

Ruby

~ Balances root chakra, overall healer, aids eyesight, confidence, mental focus, creativity, understanding of spiritual wisdom

Sapphire

~ Balances throat chakra, calming, strengthens nervous system, aids meditation and understanding of spiritual truths

Tiger Eye

~ Relieves eye diseases, aids physical energy, body intuition and development of inner strength

Topaz

~ Balances crown chakra, strengthens intuitive/psychic abilities stimulates appetite, relieves mental tension, supports hormonal balance during pregnancy and menopause

Turquoise

~ Balances throat chakra, grounding, overall healer, strengthens mind and emotions, aids meditation, grounding, reminds us of our spiritual nature

Unikite

~ Balances emotions, aids communication between inner-self and spiritual guides

Basic Healing Layouts

- ♥ Bring to the surface and dissolve fears:

  Azurite and amethyst placed on the third-eye chakra and malachite on the solar-plexus chakra

- ♥ Grounding:

  Smokey quartz placed at feet (particularly useful during healing sessions)

- ♥ Calming:

  Hold an amethyst point or a ball carved from blue quartz in the palm of the hand.

- ♥ Chakra Balancing:

  On the chakra, place a stone that naturally (not dyed) matches the color of that chakra.

  –or –

  In the palm of your client's hand, lay a piece of kyanite with the striations pointing toward their finger tips. This will balance all of their chakras at the same time.

- ♥ Bring to the surface and heal issues rooted in past-lives:

  Azurite, sugalite, and gem silica placed on the third-eye chakra and amethyst placed in the palm the hand

- ♥ Bring to the surface and calmly release emotions:

  Realgar placed on the belly chakra and amethyst on the third-eye chakra

- ♥ Heal the emotional heart:

  Rose quartz, kunzite and pink tourmaline carried together or placed together on the heart chakra

- ♥ Enhance security on the physical plane:

  Ruby or garnet placed on the base chakra and surrounded by a circle of clear quartz points with the points toward the ruby or garnet

- ♥ Enhance skill with divination, channeling or shamanic journey:

  Hold danburite while working, or lay it nearby

- ♥ Enhance skill with healing:

  Lay flint nearby while working

- ♥ Place a variety of stones around your home and your healing space to support well-being. Change them out as you feel inspired to.

Indications the stone's work is done:

- ♥ Your intuitive feel
- ♥ The stone falls off the person's body.
- ♥ After using a stone for awhile, the person forgets to use it.
- ♥ The stone disappears and can't be found.
- ♥ The stone breaks or loses its color.

My Experience With This:

When I started working with stones as healing companions, I frequently worked with them for myself. I was quite surprised to find myself easily growing into wholeness about a lot of beliefs, inner challenges, and wounds that I thought I'd be struggling with for the rest of my life.

In the years since then, I've gathered quite a variety of stones and learned how to work with each one by hanging out with it for awhile. I carry it in my pocket and sleep with it under my pillow for several days until I see how I respond to it. After that, I read what other people say about its healing properties. Then I hang out with it a bit longer, looking for how it works with the challenges other people have identified. Then I'm ready to work with it with clients.

My personal experience is that when I'm having a challenge maintaining my own wholeness, or I'm growing into something that's difficult for me, stones consistently support me more effectively than any other tool I've found.

CHAPTER 21
EMPOWERING THROUGH LANGUAGE

Our wholeness is deeply impacted by the ways we use language. Language is our tool for building bridges of understanding between people and between our own experiences and minds. Building bridges that create clarity requires accurate speaking, accurate listening, and consciousness about what's being implied in what is and isn't said.

Using language to speak full truth in kind, generous, and unconditionally loving ways makes it easy to love and celebrate ourselves and others. Using language to open ourselves to new possibilities and expand into previously unknown options creates space to consciously become more than we already know how to be. Using language to acknowledge what's already working well, what we appreciate, and what we enjoy makes it easy to create lives that are fulfilling and delightful.

Empowering statements, questions, and conversations always come from the perspective that we're involved in each of our own life experiences for a good reason and we can choose how those experiences impact us. Using language in ways that empower grounds us in the reality of the changeable nature of life on Earth and reinforces the idea that we can create the life we want.

Making this your natural way of using language will help you as a person and as a healer. Teaching it to clients will help them become fully empowered in their own lives.

Teaching Empowering Language to Clients

Weaving this into the normal flow of conversation during sessions is often the easiest way for clients to learn how to shift their own use of language.

When you hear a client say something that limits their options or casts them or someone else as a victim, wrong, or more or less powerful than another… pause the conversation and, using their words, make a statement to this effect:

I'm going to ask you to reword what you just said from…
(When someone talks to me that way I think they don't love me.)… to…
(When someone talks to me that way I choose to think they don't love me.)

Give your client space to say it the way you suggested, then point out that in their original statement, they gave the other person all the power over how they responded. They told their own mind that they had no options about their response. In the re-worded version, they acknowledged their choice, thus telling their mind that they have options about their response.

Most clients will take your suggestion and reword their statement. For those who don't, simply point out the difference between the two versions and then move on. They've heard what you said and will integrate it in their own time.

Using Language to Expand or Exclude Possibilities

Sometimes it's beneficial to speak in ways that open a wide variety of options. This makes space for exploring what's not yet known, creating from a unique point of view, and stretching beyond perceived reality.

Sometimes it's beneficial to speak in ways that tightly define something and close off additional options. This makes space for focusing on a workable collection of information and bringing it into practical action, creating something tangible, or recognizing a point of completion.

Here are some examples to inspire your thinking about this…

To help the mind access new possibilities

Replace "but" with "and"

Eliminate the use of "because"

Make "I" statements

Replace "the" with "a"

Replace "lose" with "release"

Replace "always", "can't" or "never" with "until now"

Speak in positives

Talk about what is desired with no mention of what's undesirable

Using expansive words

The following words can expand possibility by creating space for new options or opportunities, activating creative thinking, creating hope, or communicating exactly what's meant. These same words can eliminate possibility by creating indecision when decision is needed, masking what's really meant, or confusing another person.

Some expansive words:

Yes	Possible	Invite	And
Maybe	Will	Start	Both
Can	Begin	Open	All
Perhaps	Create	Dream	Anything

Using exclusive words

The following words can expand possibility by focusing attention, defining boundaries, or communicating exactly what is meant. These same words can eliminate possibility by shaming, defining reality, enforcing compliance, or masking what's really meant.

Some exclusive words:

No	Done	Right	But
Can't, cannot	Complete	Correct	Or
Wrong	Finish	Won't, will not	Forever
Impossible	Never	Don't, do not	Now

Expanding Your Awareness of How You're Using Language

Ways of speaking that support empowerment

~ Ask open-ended questions that seek an honest response from the person being asked.

~ Ask questions that include no suggestion or implication of "right" or "wrong" responses.

~ Make supportive statements.

~ Make statements that leave room for more than one perspective.

~ Make statements in which the speaker takes responsibility for their own perspectives and experiences.

Some words that empower

I ~ indicates what's being said is about the speaker's perspective, experience, or preference.

For me ~ indicates what's being said is about the speaker's perspective, experience, or preference.

Release ~ indicates choosing to let go.

And ~ supports the validity of all that is being said.

Different ~ indicates a belief in options.

More ~ indicates a focus on expanding.

Inappropriate for me ~ indicates unwillingness to participate in something and supports the free will of others.

Choose ~ acknowledges that decisions are being made and removes the option of being a victim.

Conscious ~ acknowledges awareness.

Want to ~ states a chosen desire.

Don't want to ~ states a chosen desire.

Self-empowering statements are ones in which the speaker:
- Speaks honestly about their own thoughts, feelings, and experiences.
- Makes space for the possibility of change.
- Takes responsibility for their own feelings, words, or actions.
- Acknowledges their own skills, abilities, or strengths.
- Speaks respectfully to and about their own self.

Ways of speaking that support disempowerment
- ~ Asking questions with a "correct" answer already in mind or embedded in the question.
- ~ Making derogatory or judgmental statements.
- ~ Making statements that negate the possibility or appropriateness of other perspectives or experiences.
- ~ Making statements designed to manipulate the listener.
- ~ Making statements or asking questions that assign fault, blame, guilt, or credit for one's own actions or thoughts to someone or something else.

Some words that disempower

Lose or lost ~ indicates something was removed involuntarily. Activates the belief that it should be replaced.

But ~ dismisses, excuses, or negates the validity or availability of what came before or after "but" in the sentence.

Crazy, insane ~ indicates a belief that illogical, unusual, uncomfortable, or different is inappropriate.

Less ~ indicates a focus on diminishing.

Wrong ~ indicates a belief that wrong exists.

Ashamed, shame, guilt ~ indicates a belief in the need to chastise oneself.

Need ~ disempowers when used to describe a desire. Adult needs are food, sleep, shelter and sharing love with other living beings. All else is desire.

Self-disempowering statements are ones in which the speaker:
- Hides, side-steps, overlooks, or ignores a truth.
- Speaks as though they have no options.
- Blames or credits others for their own feelings, words, skills, or actions.
- Ignores their own skills, abilities, or strengths.
- Criticizes, chastises, shames, or belittles their own self.
- Speaks as though everyone responds to a situation the same way they do.

Some indications that a speaker is disempowered or creating confusion:

~ Saying what they almost mean, and stopping short of full statements or full disclosure.

~ Speaking before they think about what they really want to say.

~ Deciding what's real about the present situation based on their own history, beliefs, or imagination.

~ Saying what they don't mean.

~ Saying something that isn't true.

~ Having a conversation in their mind that's influencing what they're saying and not sharing that inner conversation with the listener.

Some words that assign responsibility to others:

You, he, she, they ~ a statement that the words to follow are about someone other than the speaker.

Allow ~ can indicate a belief that permission must be received or given.

Should, should not, must, must not ~ indicates a belief that desires and actions have to fall within expectations or established guidelines.

Unconscious ~ indicates a belief that our minds are not under our own control.

Because ~ indicates that one thing causes another to occur.

Some ways language is used to manipulate:

Barter ~ a statement that says or insinuates the speaker should receive a favor in exchange for what they're offering.

Guilt trip ~ a statement or question implying the listener is wrong if they don't agree with the speaker or do what the speaker wants.

Insinuation ~ a statement or question that leaves the listener unclear about the speaker's position or intention.

Enticement ~ a statement or question implying a reward will be given for complying with the speaker's wishes.

CHAPTER 22
FUTURE-SELF GUIDANCE

Plan on 10 to 20 minutes for this process. This is a guided meditation process and it can only be done when the client is actively participating. It's ineffective if the client doesn't set it in motion.

Future-Self Guidance is used to support a client's ability to fully live changes they want to make in their life. The focus can be on any aspect of life, big or small. This technique is also very effective for learning how to make changes your client thinks they don't know how to make, is afraid to make, or believes to be impossible.

Our future-selves will come at our request; they're invested in us living the future they represent and they're happy to reach back in time and provide the roadmap to it. A future-self typically will not give information during the session. The guidance will come in the moments when your client is engaged in something that will either bring them closer to this future or take them further away from it. People often notice this process at work in their lives by realizing they're effortlessly making different choices than they used to.

After using this technique in a session, I teach the client how to do it on their own. I encourage them to work with this on their own to address other shifts they desire, and to reinforce their confidence when they feel discouraged about a shift they've already set in motion. I remind them that they can reconnect with any future-self they're working with as often as they want to.

The biggest challenge I see clients having is finding words to define the future-self they want to work with. Many people are more skilled at naming what they don't want than they are at naming what they do want. Many people attach their aspirations to the participation of specific people in addition to their own self, or they shape their aspirations to fit what they think is possible. I encourage clients to define future-selves who are already living what the client believes is impossible or unattainable.

It's important to focus on one future-self at a time; combining multiple desired changes makes it very difficult to clearly define any of them. Multiple changes can be worked with concurrently, just be sure to initiate each of these future-self connections in separate sessions. Some clients find if effective to work with an overall focus such as "my future-self who is absolutely delighted with all aspects of her/his life."

After doing this work, your client will gradually notice they're making decisions that are more supportive of the future they want to live. This is a very gentle, natural shift in decision making. It comes from within and generally occurs without the client having to focus on changing their behavior.

Future-Self Guidance Process

Talk with your client about the change they're trying to make until both of you can clearly and succinctly name the future-self you'll be working with, ie: my future-self who already has a child of her own. It's important for your client to word their own description of the future-self they want to receive guidance from and it's fine for you to give suggestions and help them find the description that fits perfectly for them.

When the description feels right to your client, ask them to close their eyes and keep them closed through this entire process – this is to help them stay present to self rather than interacting with you.

Give your client the following instructions, one step at a time. Pause after each step to allow your client time to complete that part:
1. Close your eyes and breathe gently, bringing yourself to center.
2. Invite your future-self who (......) to come sit with you.
3. Sit quietly for a few minutes with this future-self.
4. Whether or not you feel the presence of this future-self, ask her/him, "Please guide every action I take and every decision I make to insure that yours is the reality I live."
5. Sit quietly for a few minutes, then thank her/him for helping you.
6. Whenever you're ready, open your eyes and rejoin me here.

Give your client a minute or two to resettle and then ask how they're feeling.

My Experience With This:
Sometimes a client feels a solid, obvious connection with a future-self. Other times they don't feel the connection and may think they're doing something wrong or Future-Self Guidance won't work for them. I've noticed the client's sense of the connection doesn't change the outcome. When someone asks one of their future-selves for guidance, they consistently get the guidance.

One of My Favorite Stories About Future-Self Guidance
One of my big challenges in life has been lack of confidence about my ability to financially support myself. Throughout many years of worrying about that, I'd done a lot of inner work affirming it's ok for me to live comfortably, to earn

money from what I do best, and a variety of other related issues. The result in my life had been much work and very little change in my confidence or my financial situation.

During those years, I'd done quite a lot of future-self work with clients, some of it relating to their financial well-being. Yet it had never occurred to me to do this for myself. When it did occur to me, I worked with my future-self who has all the money she needs at all times. I didn't define a dollar amount because I knew that would change through time and what I really wanted was just to be sure there'd always be enough money when I needed it. A few days after doing that meditation, I started noticing the times when I said "no" to opportunities to earn money doing what I do best. That awareness was all I needed to shift my behavior and align with my own financial well-being.

CHAPTER 23
GROWING BEYOND LIMITATIONS

Plan on about 15 minutes for this process. This is a guided meditation process and it can only be done when the client is actively participating.

Sometimes, self-limiting decisions, beliefs, and perspectives are beneficial. They help us define what we want to do in life and they help us live that. They function like a fence around a playground – providing freedom of movement without the need to watch out for safety. When they confine someone in ways that undermine their well-being or prevent them from living their fullness, Growing Beyond Limitations is a beneficial process to use.

A simple way to notice the limits your client is living within is to listen for statements like "I can't", "I could never", "That's impossible", "I have to", etc. When your client feels expanded and supported by one of their limitations, they're using it well. When they feel confined, frustrated, blocked, or diminished by a limitation, it's a good time to grow beyond that one.

Growing Beyond Limitations Process:
Your client can do this with eyes closed or open, whichever feels best to them. Give them the following instructions, one step at a time, pausing after each so they have time to do what they need to.
1. Take a few gentle deep breaths and bring yourself to center.
2. Now hold your hands together out in front of you, palms up, forming an open basket.
3. Imagine your hands filling up with all the things you use to limit yourself. Maybe this includes your diet, responsibilities, religion, or family. Maybe it includes the weather, your health, other people's opinions, the color of your skin. Maybe it includes completely different things. Whatever they are, lovingly lay all of your self-limitations into your palm basket. Please tell me when this feels complete.
4. Now imagine a beautiful basket sitting on the floor at your feet. Choosing one thing at a time from among the things you're holding in your hands, lovingly fill the beautiful basket at your feet with each limitation you want to keep. Please tell me when this feels complete.
5. Now thank all of the limitations that are still in your palm basket for supporting you in the past. Please tell me when this feels complete.
6. Now, raise your palm basket up toward the sky and give permission for all the things that remain there to return to the universe and make themselves

available to the next person who can benefit from their help. Please tell me when this feels complete.

7. Now be with yourself for a minute and fill your heart with gratitude and love for all the tools you use to support yourself in being you. Please tell me when this feels complete.

8. If your client's eyes are closed: Whenever you're ready, please open your eyes and rejoin me here.

When your client is ready, ask how they're feeling and then gently transition to whatever comes next.

CHAPTER 24
HANDS-ON-HEALING

Plan on at least 15 minutes for this. Some situations may take up to an hour. Decide the length of the session based on the combination of your own stamina and your client's need and stamina. This is a physical contact healing process. It can be used for any physical being (human, animal, plant, etc.) who will allow you to maintain several minutes of physical touch.

Hands-on-Healing is used to heal physical, mental, emotional, or spiritual challenges. This process can be done just as well through clothing as through direct skin contact. If you've learned how to do Reiki, you already know how to do hands-on-healing. The only difference between the two is that hands-on-healing is done completely through intuitive touch and Reiki is done through established symbols and hand placements combined with intuitive touch.

It isn't necessary for your client to stay awake or focused during this type of healing. It is beneficial for you and your client to be as physically comfortable as possible.

A Simple Process for Hands-on-Healing:
1. Through observation or conversation with your client, identify at least one area of their body that appears to need healing.
2. Begin by very gently laying the palm of one of your hands on one of the areas identified. If you feel drawn to, lay both of your hands side by side or lay them on opposite sides of the area.
3. Keep your hand on that place for a few minutes, maintaining feather-light contact between your palm and your client's body. Don't massage the area or change the pressure of your hand.
4. When you feel complete with that area, move your hand to the next area that draws your attention and repeat the process. You may be drawn to another area your client has identified or to an area that you intuitively recognize. Trust yourself to follow subtle signals from your client's body.
5. Keep repeating this until you notice a sense of completion from your client's body, your client tells you they feel complete, or your attention begins to wander. Any of these things indicates your client has received what they needed.

More Ways to Do This

♥ V- spread

This is done to ease an area of condensed energy. These areas often show up as painful or the energy feels tense, thick, sticky, or dense.

After identifying an area, gently rest the back of your hand on your client's body, fingertips pointing away from you, with your index and middle fingers of that hand resting on either side of the area and your other fingers curled back away from your client. Form a V with your index and middle fingers, with the open side of the V pointing away from your body.

At an opposite point on your client's body, gently lay the back of your other hand with your middle finger extended and resting on the point. Position your finger so the tip is pointing directly toward the center of the open end of the V. Breathe and let the energy run between your finger and the V for several minutes until you feel a sense of completion.

♥ Aura Smoothing

This is done to ease emotional intensity or physical pain, and to support full integration after bodywork or energywork.

Keep your hands about six inches away from your client's body with your palms toward your client. Starting at the top of their head and moving down to their toes, slowly and gently float your hands down the length of their body, arms, and legs. Repeat this a few times until you feel a sense of completion.

♥   Aura Fluffing

This is done to ease emotional or mental intensity and to support spaciousness in the aura.

Keeping your hands about twelve inches away from your client with your palms facing away from them, gently lift their energy away from their body as if you were lifting palms full of feathers. Do this over the whole length of their body and around all sides, moving in any direction that feels right to you. Repeat this a few times until you feel a lightness in their energy.

My Experience With This:

I notice areas that can benefit from Hands-on-Healing by listening to what my client tells me, by feeling a draw to an area, or by feeling pressure against my palm when I hold it near an area. For me, a sense of completion with the work feels like the person's energy is full, my hand has become quiet and still, or my mind is wandering rather than staying focused.

Some of My Favorite Stories About Hands-On-Healing

Two days before he hosted dinner for our group of friends, one of my friends cut his palm pretty badly. After dinner he was rubbing it and mentioned it was infected and getting very sore. I reached over and gently held his hand between both of my palms for about 20 minutes while we all continued visiting. When he pulled his hand away, the pain, infection, and swelling were all gone and he was able to use his hand normally. When he woke up the next morning he noticed the cut was almost completely healed.

My grandpa was very good at healing headaches and did this for me a few times. He'd put the tip of his index finger on my temple, put another finger on the front of my forehead, and hold his fingers still for a few minutes. Even migraines disappeared completely when he did this.

My cat developed an abscess after getting into a tangle with another cat. I couldn't take him to a vet when I noticed the abscess so I sat down beside him and cupped his hip in the palm of my hand for about thirty minutes while I watched TV. When I removed my hand, the cut had completely disappeared and the lump was considerably smaller. The next morning the lump had disappeared and Mister was back to normal.

During a class I was taking, the teacher asked us all to gather around while she demonstrated one of the techniques. Another student in the class had a tooth that had physically shifted position and it was bothering him. The teacher put both of her middle fingers inside his mouth and rested them gently against opposite sides of his tooth. She held her fingers there, not moving them at all, for about three minutes. Every one of us in the class watched with a bit of awe as our classmate's tooth moved back into its original position and stayed there. When we finished the class a few months later his tooth was still in its correct position.

CHAPTER 25
INTERSPECIES COMMUNICATION & HEALING

This is often called Animal Communication. I prefer to use the term Interspecies Communication because the same intuitive skills are used to communicate with all beings who aren't human. Intuitively communicating with other species is done exactly the same way as having intuitive interactions with people.

The primary challenges to clear communication with other species living here on Earth are the physical language barrier and the assumptions we humans make about their intelligence and their roles in relation to us. Intuitive conversations completely clear the language barrier. The assumption challenges are completely cleared by interacting with them as the individuals they are and respecting their free-will just as much as you do with humans. Each one is a unique soul with their own life purpose and they're as fully conscious and connected with spirit as anyone else here on Earth.

For healing purposes, communication is done through a combination of touch, intuitive conversations, and observing behavior and body language. Particularly in situations where the healing is focused on behavior or emotion, or is for a soul who doesn't live on Earth, it's very effective to work completely through intuitive conversations. Most of the healing techniques in this book can be used with anyone living on Earth. When doing guided meditation processes with animals, it's helpful for a person to do the meditation while touching the animal or focusing on them.

My Experience With This:
Intuitively within my mind, I hear beings other than human fluently speaking English. I keep this skill fresh by interacting daily with the "others" I encounter. These conversations are typically about very mundane things.... saying good morning to a flower, stone, bird, spider, raccoon, etc. and pausing for a few seconds to receive their responses. I also chat with my cats while we do our daily activities and pause for a few seconds to receive their responses. Pausing for a few seconds and taking that time to listen with my heart is a key part of these conversations for me.

When I'm doing healing work with another species I pause until I receive their response, which may be considerably longer than a few seconds. Sometimes it's as difficult for them to describe the root of their challenge or to align with their wholeness as it is for humans. For me, listening fully is key to being able to fully support their wholeness.

Some of My Favorite Interspecies Adventures

Everyday Conversations

On a daily basis I have reciprocal conversations with whoever I encounter in physical form. Regardless of the physical form another is living in, I consider them to be a cousin, a friend, a neighbor. Sometimes I initiate the conversations, sometimes they do. When tending to my gardens I talk with the insects, plants, and trees living there – appreciating their beauty, asking about their well-being, and receiving their loving attention. When a storm comes in I talk with the wind, thunder, lightning, rain, or snow. Birds and animals are my constant companions and we talk frequently as we go about our daily activities. The richness of these relationships and the easy flow of sharing that nourishes each of us constantly reminds me how closely related we all are.

Hummingbird

I walked into the local grocery store one hot Sunday afternoon and saw something flit by my face. Looking down, I saw a distressed hummingbird laying at my feet. After gently scooping her into my palm, I took her outside and set her in a shaded flower pot, then went back inside and asked the folks at the bakery for a little water and sugar. Returning outside I found her still in the flower pot, breathing shallowly. I gave her the sugar water and watched from a protective distance while she slowly drank all of it and started acting a bit more normal. Leaving her alone, I did my shopping and returned about twenty minutes later to see her fly from the flower pot to an overhead wire, then off to wherever she went.

I've always had a special love for hummingbirds. While someone else may have also noticed her before she died, and known how to help her, I'm grateful and amazed at the synchronicity of her falling at my feet and me knowing exactly how to help her.

Garden Song and Dance

I love to garden and many years ago, after a good long day of planting, I started spontaneously dancing through my gardens singing "grow little plants grow!" Although this was very odd behavior for me at the time, I was enjoying the day and my own silliness so I kept playfully dancing and singing whatever made up tune came to mind. When I finished with my gardens, I sang and danced for all the trees in my yard and was quite surprised when I noticed shimmering light in the tree leaves. I stopped, rubbed my eyes, and looked again. The trees were still shimmering. I didn't know what to make of it so I sang and danced for awhile longer and just kept enjoying my silliness. A few weeks later, I woke up to a beautiful morning and headed out to my gardens. Before doing anything else, and just to satisfy my own skepticism, I checked the trees for shimmering light and didn't see any. So I started dancing and singing to my gardens again and the next time I looked at the trees, the leaves were shimmering. After experiencing this for many years and at my homes in four different states, I mentioned it in a conversation with a Hawaiian woman I knew. She laughed and told me that Hawaiian Kahunas go out to the forest before ceremonies and sing to the trees until they shimmer back to them. As with many of my early adventures with these things, I was delighted and humbled to learn that I'd spontaneously remembered how to communicate with another group of our Earth cousins. And yes, I still sing and dance for my gardens and trees and the tree leaves still shimmer with me!

CHAPTER 26
INTUITIVE READINGS & CHANNELING

For healing purposes, these are methods used to discern and provide insights or information that support constructive growth, healing, or consciousness on the physical plane. There are numerous ways to channel and do readings. Books, information, and classes about how to develop these skills are readily available online and sometimes locally.

Providing Intuitive Readings for Clients

All intuitive skills can become ways of receiving messages for other people. Here are a few guidelines to follow if you deliver any of those messages:

♥ If you're not certain a message you received is accurate, silently ask, "Is this true?" Feel for the answer at your solar-plexus. If the message feels true in your own body, share it and ask your client if it feels true to them or makes sense to them. A message that you don't understand may make complete sense to your client.

♥ If a message you deliver doesn't feel accurate to your client, let it drop. You may have interpreted it wrong, it may make sense at another time, or it may belong to someone else.

♥ If you're hesitant about delivering a message, pause for a second and tell spirit something to this effect: "If this message is mine to deliver, please give me the words when the recipient is ready to receive them with the love with which they're given." Then let go of the message and move on; if it's yours to deliver the right words will be there at the right time.

♥ If you're unable to deliver a message, please remember there are many messengers and when the time is right the message will get to the person it's meant for.

My Experience With This:

When I've delivered a message accurately it usually makes sense to the recipient. It may make sense in ways they can talk about or it may feel right in some unexplainable way. When I'm inaccurate, typically it's because of one of the following dynamics:

● I delivered the message to the wrong person.

When this happens the message doesn't make sense to the person I delivered it to and we let it go. People have come back to me later and told me they talked about the message with someone else and it turned out to be for that person.

- I delivered the message before my client was consciously aware of what it addressed.

    When this happens, happens, the person doesn't connect with the message and we let it go. People have come back to me months or years later and told they finally understand the message.

- I interpreted the message through my own filters.

    When this happens, the message sort of makes sense to my client, and something feels out of place. So we talk about it until both of us understand the real message. In these situations, I explain that I was looking through my own perspectives and I thank my client for knowing their own truth and staying with their truth while we discovered the real message. I explain this because I want people to know that accessing their own wisdom is much more significant in their life than anything I tell them.

Here are some methods for doing readings and channeling:

Astrology

    The practice of reading charts of planetary locations and movements and their impact on a person based on where the planets were when the person was born (natal chart) and how their current position relates to the person's natal chart.

Divining rods

    Copper rods or Y shaped branches that are used to discern both physical and spiritual energies. In healing they're often used to find energy blockages within the body or aura.

I-ching

    Coins that are tossed and then read to receive insights.

Muscle Testing

    This is also called Kinesiology. It's a way of working with the strength or weakness of muscles in response to a specific question, thought, or substance. For healing this is usually used to gather information about what a person's body needs in terms of nutrition, relief, or adjustment.

Numerology

    The practice of working the esoteric meanings of numbers and the ways they relate to each other.

Palmistry

    Reading the lines on people's hands or feet and the shapes of their fingers and palms or toes and soles. For healing, it's used to discern intentions, motivations, and innate skills, challenges and characteristics.

Pendulums

> Freely swinging weights that are used to discern energy in and around living beings.

Runes

> Carved stones or cards with symbols on them from ancient Gaelic languages. They're used to receive insights.

Tarot & other cards

> Decks of cards with images on them. They're used to receive insights.

Tea leaves

> Ordinary tea leaves that settle into the bottom of a cup when they've been made into tea. They're used to receive insights for the person who drank that cup of tea.

Trance

> A form of deep meditation that's typically used by people who want to make sure their conscious mind doesn't influence the information they channel from spirit.

Spirit Communication

This is sometimes called Mediumship. It's typically a form of channeling that facilitates direct conversations between souls on the spirit plane and living people. It can also be used to facilitate conversations with living people who have disabilities that prevent them from consciously communicating, such as a coma. As a healer, your role if you choose to offer spirit communication is to receive words or images from those on the spirit plane and deliver them to those on the physical plane. This is usually done by allowing the soul to speak and then repeating exactly what they said, by interpreting or paraphrasing what they said, or by allowing the soul to speak directly through you.

Some of the ways Spirit Communication is used for healing and growth:
* Gathering understandable information about what's needed to re-balance specific challenges or to grow in specific ways.
* Helping loved ones who are separated by death develop their new form of relationship, heal their grief, and continue relating to each other.
* Discovering internalized blockages and new focuses for growth.
* Helping clients develop their own relationships with their spirit guides.

My Experience With This:
When I engage in spirit communication on behalf of a living person, I begin with thought speaking with the soul on the spirit side. Once the connection is solid, I speak the exact words I receive if the soul wants the living person to

hear all of their words. If the soul prefers that I interpret what they're saying, I continue speaking with the soul through thought and I speak with the living person out loud.

- When a soul prefers that I interpret, I typically experience at least one or more of these dynamics:
  - They speak very slowly, with pauses between the words.
  - They have a hard time finding their words.
  - They stop talking when I stop talking.
  - They stand a little behind me.
  - I get the thought or feel that they want me to do the talking.
- When a soul prefers to speak directly:
  - I get the thought or feel that they want to speak directly.
  - They stand beside me or between me and the person I'm working with.
  - They stop talking when I try to interpret what they say.

CHAPTER 27
RECOGNIZING RIGHT TIMING

When your client struggles to accomplish things, or frequently experiences push-back from others, they'll benefit by being able to recognize the difference between the open flow of energy when they're aligned with right timing and the resistant energy when they're not aligned.

Ways to help your clients recognize right timing:

♥ Ask your client to focus on something they know they can do and to pay attention to how their body responds to that. Their body will respond the same way when they're aligned with right timing.

Then ask them to focus on something they know they can't do and to pay attention to how their body responds to that. Their body will respond the same way when they're not aligned with right timing.

♥ Guide your client through the process for using their body as a pendulum.

My experience with this:
When I'm aligned with right timing I feel at ease about what I'm doing or saying. It's easy to connect with anyone I need to and our communication flows well.

When I'm out of alignment with right timing I experience at least one of the following:

- I don't have time in the moment and I forget about it later.
- I'm concerned about the response or reaction I'll receive from others.
- I feel the desire or need to wait and let the situation develop more fully.
- Regardless of how I try, it doesn't come together.

CHAPTER 28
LYMPH SYSTEM DRAIN

Plan on 30 minutes for this. This is a physical bodywork technique that's done to strengthen the immune system, relieve allergies, and heal viral and bacterial infections. For infections, it's most efficient when it's done as soon as symptoms appear. This is easiest to do when your client is wearing one layer of lightweight clothing or no clothing.

Process for Lymph System Drain
1. Massage soles of both feet.
2. Using your fingers, stimulate the points in the web between each of the fingers and toes.
3. Using your fingers, stimulate the liver and kidneys by pressing the points on the outside of each calf and thigh.
4. Press your elbow firmly into each sciatic point and release when the discomfort in the point subsides.
5. Press your elbow firmly into each rear hip point and release when the discomfort in the point subsides.
6. Using your fingers, stimulate the points along both sides of the spine by pressing approximately every two inches from the top of the hips to the base of neck.
7. Using your fingers, stimulate the points on each shoulder blade.
8. Using your fingers, gently stimulate the pelvic points by pressing on them.
9. Using your fingers, stimulate the front hip points by pressing on them.
10. Using your fingers, rake the back on each side, moving along the rib cage from the spine to the front of the sides. This is easiest to do while your client is laying on their back and you're reaching across their body and under they back on the side opposite side of where you are.
11. Gently massage around each breast using a kneading motion and working from all directions.
12. Firmly squeeze under each arm pit three or four times.
13. Using your fingers, press into and pump the points below the collar bones and shoulder joints.
14. Using your fingers, stimulate the points along the top of the collar bones by pressing approximately every inch from the shoulder to the center of the collar bones.
15. Using your hands, "milk" down to the belly using long deep strokes from the collar bones to the belly around and between the breasts.

16. Using your hands, do a Sun/Moon massage on the belly.

    Starting at the top of the right hip, push down and massage the colon in a circular motion moving from the right hip up toward the ribs on the right, then across toward the ribs on the left and down to the left hip. Then move down toward the top of the pelvis and across the top of the pelvic bone then up toward the right hip. Repeat this several times, working as deeply as is comfortable for your client.

17. Firmly squeeze each shoulder from the top.

18. Firmly squeeze the lymph nodes under the chin.

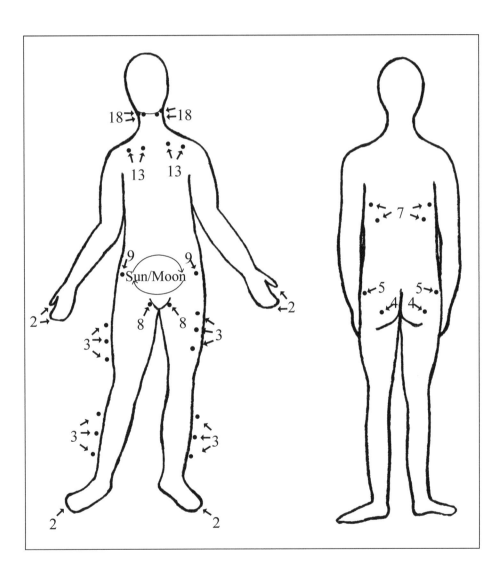

CHAPTER 29
RELEASING TEACHERS

Plan on 10 - 20 minutes for this process. This is a guided meditation process and it can only be done when the client is actively participating.

We all carry some lessons about being human in this life that no longer serve us well. Those lessons may have come from parents or other relatives, friends, life experiences, or somewhere else. Those teachers may be named poverty, war, broken leg, Dad, racism, Grandma, ex-girlfriend, religion, school… Whoever those teachers are, we absorbed their teachings because they were somehow beneficial to us at the time. Continuing to learn from them, or pass their lessons on to others, is completely optional. Naming the teachers and lovingly releasing them helps us release the aspects of their teachings that are no longer aligned with the person we choose to be.

For people who continue to say, do, or believe things they no longer want in their lives, Releasing Teachers can be very beneficial. If your client can't readily name where they learned the things they continue to do, talk with them until both of you know how to name that teacher.

In the instructions below, I use Poverty as the name of the teacher. Please use the name your client identified.

Releasing Teachers Process:
Give your client the following instructions, one step at a time, pausing after each to give them the time they need:
1. Close your eyes and breathe gently, bringing yourself to center.
2. Now invite Poverty to come sit with you as your honored guest. Please let me know when she/he is here.
3. Now thank Poverty for all that you've learned from her/him. Please tell me when this feels complete.
4. Now tell Poverty that you'll be your own teacher from here forward and she/he is released from all responsibility to teach you anything more. Please tell me when that feels complete.
5. Now tell Poverty that she/he is free to share their wisdom with whoever will benefit from it next. Then watch quietly while Poverty moves away from you and completely disappears. Please tell me when this feels complete.
6. Whenever you're ready, please open your eyes and rejoin me here.

Give your client a minute or two to settle and then ask how they're feeling.

My Experience With This

When someone isn't walking their talk I know they're participating in a way of being they don't fully align with. This shows up very easily when the person's behavior doesn't match the ideals or values they talk about.

When I notice this in a session, I look for the teacher's name by listening for who or what my client talks about in relation to the dynamic. Because embedded lessons often grow into undefinable motivations, I find that personifying the teacher, even if they're not human, helps people embrace their own power in relation to those embedded lessons. That makes it much easier to fully live beyond the lessons and into the true wisdoms and gifts those lessons brought.

CHAPTER 30
SOUL RETRIEVAL

Plan on 20 - 45 minutes for this process. This is a guided meditation process and it can only be done when the client actively participates in it. If desired, this can be accompanied by a "heartbeat" drum beat… this is a simple 1, 2, 3, 4 drum beat that's repeated without variation.

Soul Retrieval is done to help people return to wholeness. It's used after trauma – which can be any deeply upsetting experience the person hasn't yet been able to integrate into their being. In addition to being used to heal from specific traumas, Soul Retrieval is an effective healing process for post traumatic stress.

The shamanic perspective supporting this process is that when we have an experience we can't emotionally or intellectually integrate at the time it happens, we leave a little bit of our energy living in that moment. That piece of our energy takes care of the memory so we can continue growing to the point where we can integrate the experience. If we forget to bring our energy back together, those pieces of our energy live permanently in the experience and eventually become self-defeating dynamics.

When memories of the experience(s) have been forgotten, compartmentalized, or submerged the aftermath of trauma often shows up as lack of memory from periods of time. It can also show as memories that are controlled, shut down or pushed away when they come to consciousness or as persistent self-defeating or self-abusive behaviors and repeated aversions to, or anxiety about, specific types of experiences or situations.

Your Role Before Beginning the Soul Retrieval:
- ♥ Listen carefully when a client is telling you what's on their mind, most people will readily name their traumas.
- ♥ When listening to your client's trauma story, stay emotionally detached.
    To support yourself in this, notice when your emotions get engaged or when you want to stop listening. This may show up as a desire to comfort the person, tears of your own, or you feeling emotions such as anger, fear, or pain. Any of these are indications that something within you needs healing. Take a gentle breath and re-center yourself. After the session is over, tend to healing this as soon as you have time.
- ♥ Listen for the root point of trauma.

Regardless of the name attached to the trauma (rape, combat, death, car accident, illness, etc.), the root you're looking for is the shocking awareness your client received when the trauma occurred.

Here are some examples:
- My body can be damaged by another person.
- My body can fail me.
- I can be controlled by something other than me.
- I'm capable of killing.
- People I love go away.
- I'm capable of hurting someone else.
- I'm on my own.
- I'm powerless in some situations.

♥ Throughout this whole process, please remember ~

Your client will be touching very painful memories and may want to distract their focus away from the pain by interacting with you. To strengthen their ability to stay present to their memories, I find it helpful to do this type of healing without physically touching the person.

♥ Another form of distraction is to change the topic.

When that happens, I ask if the client feels complete with what we were just discussing. If they do, I don't pursue it any further unless they come back to it.

♥ Fully accept your client's interpretation of the experience.

The actual details of the experience may or may not match your client's memory of what happened. That's ok – their trauma is anchored into their interpretation of the experience and that's the doorway into healing.

♥ Although several traumas may be discussed during a session, focus on one trauma for the current Soul Retrieval and leave the others for other sessions.

♥ Any of these are indications that it's time to shift into the Soul Retrieval:
- You're able to name the root trauma.
- Your client starts repeating what's already been said.
- Your client gets lost in emotion.
- Your client goes silent.

Your Role During the Soul Retrieval:

In addition to guiding your client through the process listed below, please keep these things in mind:

♥ When naming the original trauma your client will be connecting with, use the description of the root point of trauma.

Example: The first moment you were aware that your body can fail you.

♥ You'll lead and follow your client in this process.
  ~ When you're giving instructions, you're in the lead.
  ~ When your client is working with what you asked her/him to do, they're in the lead.
  ~ Wait for your client to tell you they feel complete before you give them the next step of the process.
♥ Sometimes a client will try to distance from their emotions by telling you what they're experiencing.

  When this happens, gently re-direct their attention to their own process. I do this by gently saying something like, "Please stay with yourself and silently receive all that this part of you is sharing. Just let me know when that feels complete."
♥ A Soul Retrieval is a profound act of self-love.

  This may be your client's first experience of fully accepting their own truth and they may experience a lot of emotion in the process. Please support them with plenty of tissues and with the tenderness of your unconditional love.

Process for Soul Retrieval:

When guiding a client through this process, ask them to keep their eyes closed, silently receive, and verbally tell you when they feel complete with each step of the process. This is to help them stay present to self rather than interacting with you, and it allows them to have all the time they need rather than fitting into your sense of timing.

Give your client the following instructions, one step at a time:

1. Keeping your eyes closed, slowly move back in time to the first moment you were aware that (…description of the root point of trauma…). You don't need to be able to identify the time or to name or describe the experience. Just keep moving further and further back until you feel like you've reached that moment. When you're there, please tell me.

2. Now ask the part of you who's living in that moment to come sit with you and tell you her/his story. You may receive words, emotions, images, whole thoughts, or general impressions. Whatever you receive is fine. Just silently receive and if emotions come up, let yourself feel them. Please tell me when this feels complete.

3. Thank this part of you for her/his honesty and ask if she/he is ready to come home to your heart, finish growing up, and rejoin you at the age you are now as a positive, supportive part of your being. Please tell me what she/he says.

4. If the answer is "no", tell your client:

> Gently tell this part of you that's ok, they're welcome to come home to your heart whenever they're ready. Please tell me this feels complete.

5. If the answer is "yes", tell your client:

> Now physically open your arms wide like you're welcoming someone in for a hug. Breathe into your heart and invite this part of you to come in through your heart and settle into your body however she/he needs to. Please tell me when this feels complete.

6. Now call to you all of the girls and women (boys and men) within you who have been protecting this aspect of you. Please tell me when it feels like everyone is here.

7. Ask them all to tell you their stories. They can all talk at once, you can absorb that. Just silently receive what they share. If emotions come up, let yourself feel them. Please tell me when this feels complete.

8. Thank them all for their honesty and ask if they're ready to come home to your heart, finish growing up, and rejoin you at the age you are now as positive, supportive parts of your being. Please tell me how they respond.

9. For any who answer "no", tell your client:

> Gently tell them that's ok and they're welcome to come home to your heart whenever they're ready.

10. For any who answer "yes", tell your client:

> Now physically open your arms wide like you're welcoming someone in for a hug, breathe into your heart, and invite all these aspects of you to come in through your heart and settle into your body however they need to. Please tell me when this feels complete.

11. Take a deep breath and whenever you're ready, please open your eyes and rejoin me here.

After your client opens their eyes, give them a minute or so to settle in and then ask how they're feeling. If you perceive any loose threads of energy that need to be healed, take a few minutes and discuss those threads with your client. If talking about the threads doesn't give your client a sense of completion, ask her/him to give those threads permission to come home to her/his heart and synthesize into her/his being in ways that support your client's wholeness. Then let your client know it may take a few weeks for these loose threads to completely synthesize and all that's left for her/him to do about it is to be patient and loving with their own process. Then move gently to another focus in the session. If you're at the end of the session, take a few minutes to just be with your client and support her/him in grounding. Then end the session.

Please Let Your Client Know:
After receiving this type of healing, it takes about 48 hours for the energy to completely settle. Soaking for 20 minutes in a warm bath with lemon oil or juice, rosemary oil, or cedar oil added to the water will help their energy settle more quickly and gently.

During these 48 hours their emotions may be all over the place and that's ok. Ask them to not make decisions or relate to anyone based on their emotions during this time period. They need to just notice what they're feeling and let it be. Their emotions will settle by the time 48 hours have passed.

Within a few days they'll start noticing shifts in their ways of being and the healing will continue to gently and naturally unfold for the next several months.

My Experience With This:
When people have a hard time understanding the concept of leaving a piece of their energy living in the moment of trauma, I find it helpful to explain it as being like a bookmark – it's something we leave in place so we'll remember to go back and do more with it.

When they find it difficult to understand why or how that bookmark becomes self-defeating behavior, I talk about how frustrating it would be for anyone to live the same moment, over and over again for years or decades, with no ability to experience anything else.

When I find myself wanting to comfort or soothe someone during a soul retrieval, I find it helpful to remind myself that the person they're really longing for is their own self. My job is to help them access their ability to fully embrace everything about them and their life. This means that I reserve hugs and empathetic comments for the times before or after the soul retrieval. During the soul retrieval, I support their personal power by letting them be present to their own discomfort until they find their balance within it.

Each one of us experiences moments in which we're the only one available to deal with what's happening. If we're out of balance when this occurs, we need to be able to heal ourselves. Having experienced someone else trusting us to handle our own emotions supports our ability to heal ourselves when no one else is available to help.

One of My Favorite Stories About Soul Retrieval

A woman came to see me after she'd struggled for decades with periodic spells of "out of character" behavior. Overall her adult life was happy, she was healthy, and she had a strong circle of friends and family. Every now and again she'd intentionally offend or alienate people she cared about, then work hard and successfully restore those relationships. She was usually very kind and generous and couldn't understand why she did that.

As we talked, she mentioned having been trapped in a neighborhood tree fort by a couple of kids she was friends with when they were all in elementary school. They kept her there for a few hours and she couldn't remember anything happening other than not being able to leave when she wanted to. We talked about the possibility that the tree fort experience may be the root of her "out of character" behavior, and she decided to try a soul retrieval.

During her soul retrieval she found herself back in the treehouse, holding the door shut while her best friend and another girl cried and tried to get out. Staying with the information she was receiving was very hard for her. We lingered in this part of the process for quite awhile until she was ready to continue.

The end result was that she realized she'd trapped the two girls because she was jealous of their friendship with each other. She knew she was scaring them by blocking the door and she'd been happy about doing that. The root of her trauma turned out to be her awareness that she could be cruel. She realized her "out of character behavior" in adulthood had been her attempts to remember what really happened in the tree fort and do something to heal her tendency toward jealousy and her defenses when she felt jealous. Over the next several months, she successfully healed her dance with jealousy and fully restored her ability to be kind to the people she loved.

CHAPTER 31
WORKING WITH OTHER LIFETIMES

Some of the agendas we carry into each lifetime are karmic; they originate in other lifetimes and we've chosen to do more with them this time around. We use karma to help us stay focused on growing and fulfilling our purpose for the whole series of lifetimes we have on Earth. It's a tool we use to remind ourselves which threads still require our loving attention.

We also carry agendas from past-lives, for future-lives, and for the here and now. These include things we want to make sure we complete during this lifetime such as skills we want to perfect and unfinished experiences from other lives. They include things we want to continue developing in this lifetime such as relationships, visions, and wisdoms we want to anchor on Earth for future generations. They include foundations we want to put in place for our own future lifetimes such as developing or expanding skills we'll need and participating in experiences that support a future-life purpose.

The reasons for working with other lifetimes are personal exploration or growth, and healing something that diminishes well-being in this lifetime. When we experience something connected to another lifetime and it inspires us or it enhances our current life, it's an invitation to enjoy a broader range of our own lived experiences. When we experience something that's upsetting or disruptive to our current life, it's an invitation to support our long-term well-being by finishing some unfinished business.

Some of the techniques used to work with other lifetimes include shamanic journey, meditation, intuitive readings, past-life regression, and some forms of bodywork and energy balancing. I encourage you to explore several techniques and then choose ones that flow easily for you.

Past-Lives

When residual imbalances from past-lives need to be healed, they tend to show up as recurrent issues or disruptive patterns that don't have identifiable points of origin in the current lifetime. They may also show up as consistent revulsion or attraction to a specific person, place, object, or type of experience that has no identifiable cause in the current lifetime.

Some examples are: addictions, repeated attraction to destructive or painful relationships or behaviors, obsessions, chronic lack of personal power, chronic fears, repetitive failures or disruptions, etc.

Noticing past-life imbalances

One way to notice these imbalances is to listen deeply and feel intuitively when your client tells you why they've come for a session. Ask when the issue started and if they know how or why it started. If their explanation feels ancient, a bit less than solid, or it's something they've explored in-depth without feeling satisfied they've defined it, the imbalance probably originates in a previous life.

Another way to notice this is to use a divination tool such as tarot cards.

> Tarot cards most likely to indicate past-life imbalances:
> > 6 of Cups, Judgement
> Tarot cards most likely to indicate the need for healing:
> > Princess of Cups, Temperance
> Tarot cards most likely to indicate full resolution of imbalances:
> > Justice, The World, Death

My Experience With This:

I feel a slight hollowness or transparency in memories from other lifetimes; it's like they're an echo. They're definitely more substantial than imaginary things, which feel like they could float away or I could reach right through them. They're not quite as solid as current life experiential memories; which feel a bit weighty and sit solidly where they are.

In the presence of a past-life dynamic that needs healing, I feel like a jagged edge just revealed itself. The connection between the current life challenge and past-life dynamic makes sense and I can usually fully articulate how and why they're connected.

In the presence of a past-life dynamic that doesn't need healing, I feel like a puzzle piece just fell perfectly into place. I can usually articulate how it supports well-being in the current lifetime.

Indications that past-life completion will be helpful

♥ A challenge, struggle, or issue isn't fully explainable by circumstances or events in the current life and it persists regardless of receiving appropriate health care, skill building, or emotional, intellectual, and spiritual growth.

♥ The person decides they're ready to grow beyond the need to live within karma. Eventually we develop our own skills to a level that supports our ability to stay on course without using karma to remind ourselves. When we get to this point, we know it and we typically choose to finish up all of our loose karmic threads and stop creating new ones.

Past-Life Regression Process

Plan on taking 30 - 45 minutes with this. This is a guided meditation designed to help people remember past-lives. If you're inclined to do so, your client may benefit from you recording their regression or giving them written notes about what they tell you during this process.

To use this for growth and spiritual exploration, focus on any lifetimes your client taps into. To use this for healing, focus on the lifetime that's the source of the challenge your client is working with.

Give your client the following instructions, one step at a time, pausing after each to give them the time they need:

1. Close your eyes, take a gentle deep breath, and bring yourself to center.
2. Keeping your eyes closed, look for the red cloud. When you find it, step onto it and sit in a comfortable position.
   - For healing use this statement: Keeping your eyes closed, look for the red cloud that will take you to the lifetime at the root of your (…name of the challenge).
3. Relax as the cloud begins floating upward, slowly changing color to orange.
4. Continue relaxing as the cloud rises higher and changes color to yellow.
5. Breathe and relax as the cloud rises still higher and changes color to green.
6. Continue relaxing and begin looking around as the color of the cloud changes to blue.
7. Breathe and relax as the cloud changes color to purple and slowly comes to a stop.
8. Step off of your cloud and look down at your feet.
9. Please tell me what you see or feel around you.
10. ♥♥♥ Now it's time for you – the healer – to adlib a bit. Ask your client questions that will help them orient to the environment the cloud took them to. Ask questions that don't lead their response in any way – make no suggestions or assumptions about their species, body, location, or what may be around them. Pause for several seconds after each question so your client has time to observe and find words.

    Some good places to start:
    - Please describe your feet to me.
    - Beginning at your feet, please tell me about your legs and your body.
    - Can you tell me how old you are?
    - Can you hear anyone calling your name?
        (if yes…. Can you tell me who's calling you?)
    - Do you see where you live?

(if yes… Can you describe your home to me?)

    - Do you see anyone you know?

(if yes… Can you tell me who that is?)

11. When you feel your client is oriented, ask them to begin moving toward something that catches their attention.

12. Now ask your client to tell you what they're seeing or feeling.

13. ♥♥♥ Beginning here, you'll lead your client only by asking questions that encourage them to share more information about something they said that caught your attention, or about something they indicated was interesting to them. Always follow your client's lead with this – don't try to interpret what they say, don't add your thoughts or insights into the conversation, and don't try to correct how they word anything. Just use what they tell you to form your next question or statement in a way that encourages them to continue exploring.

When you feel that your client has gotten all the available information, or you feel the energy dissipating, guide your client back to the present with these instructions:

14. Now look for your purple cloud and when you find it, step onto it and sit in a comfortable position.

15. Relax as the cloud begins floating upward, slowly changing color to blue.

16. Continue relaxing as the cloud rises higher and changes color to green.

17. Breathe and relax as the cloud begins to float down toward Earth and changes color to yellow.

18. Continue relaxing and begin looking around as the cloud floats lower and changes color to orange.

19. Breathe and relax as the cloud changes color to red, gently rests on the Earth and comes to a stop.

20. Whenever you're ready, take a slow deep breath, open your eyes, and rejoin me here.

21. After your client has returned, talk about their experience and share any insights you received.

If this regression was done for healing, give your client the instructions for the self-guided Past-Life Completion process on page 205. Ask them to do that process within the next two or three nights.

Concurrent-Lives

These are different lifetimes that are being lived by the same soul at the same time; they're also called parallel lives. Most of us spontaneously shift between concurrent lives from time to time and experience those shifts as moments of déjà-vu that may feel odd, but don't impact our current life.

Sometimes a concurrent life can help resolve challenges in the current lifetime – the lifetime your client is fully aware of. A simple way to do this is to ask your client to imagine and absorb a reality in which the challenge is resolved or isn't present at all.

A way to guide your client into this is to give them these instructions, one step at a time:

1. Close your eyes, take a gentle deep breath and bring yourself to center.
2. Keeping your eyes closed, imagine yourself living… (name the desired outcome of whatever your client is trying to resolve).
3. Still keeping your eyes closed, point to the place in this room where that reality already exists.
4. Now, open your eyes and walk to that place.
5. Please pause there and let yourself absorb that energy until you feel full.
6. Whenever you're ready, open your eyes and rejoin me here.

When a concurrent life is creating challenges, the indications often look like bi-polar disorder, dissociative identity disorder, or schizophrenia. The way to discern between a potential mental illness and a concurrent life is in the behavior of your client. When the issue is a concurrent life, your client will be able to stay fully grounded, present, and functional whenever they need to.

If you feel your client has concurrent life challenges, a good approach is to ask them what's attractive or disturbing about the concurrent life. If they can't name those things, using Tarot or some other form of divination can help identify them. When the dynamics have been identified, help your client find ways to bring the attractive things into their current life or ways to heal the disturbance they feel about the other life.

A way to guide your client into this is to give them these instructions, one step at a time:

1. Close your eyes, take a gentle deep breath and bring yourself to center.
2. Now give yourself permission to enjoy and absorb all that you love about that alternate life and to release all that disturbs you about it. Please tell me when this feels complete.
3. Whenever you're ready, open your eyes and rejoin me here.

Future-Lives

Whispers of future-lives are present for most people; it's normal for them to show up as visions, dreams, or hopes that are enjoyed and never acted on. The only time I've noticed future-lives causing challenges that need healing is when someone misunderstands the timing of a future event and creates an imbalance as a result of trying to make it happen too soon. When this occurs, the person usually feels the solidity and certainty of whatever it is and can't understand their inability to make it happen. Sometimes this looks like an obsession or like the person is disconnected from reality.

Indications of Future-Life Challenges

♥ A person is so certain something specific is going to happen that they keep trying until they're out of balance.

♥ One person can't let go of the idea that a relationship is long term or of a specific nature and the other person disagrees.

When you feel that a client is challenged by a future-life, an effective way to address that is to teach them how to recognize right timing. Here's a simple way to do that:

1. Ask your client to close their eyes, take a few gentle breaths, and focus on the situation that's challenging them.
2. Now ask them to pay attention to how their body responds to each time frame you're going to mention.
3. Begin with a statement such as, "is that going to happen in…" then slowly move forward and backward randomly, naming different time frames.
   Example: 1 year, 60 years, 2 months, 5 years, never, 300 years…
4. Pause at each time frame and give your client a few seconds to feel it and tell you what they feel. Keep track of your client's responses.
5. If your client finds a time frame their body aligns with, that's right timing. If they don't find right timing, there are still too many variables at play to discern when or if they'll actually do whatever it is.
   Some ways our bodies show alignment with right timing:
   - A strong feeling of "yes" or "right fit"
   - Shift into sustained enthusiasm or excitement
   - Shift into deep relaxation
   - Leaning forward

One of My Favorite Past-Life Adventures

The first time I explored past-lives was in a workshop with about twenty other people. I'd read about past-lives, and even seen a few movies about them, and I was a bit skeptical. My sweetie and I sat together, both of us pretty sure we couldn't be hypnotized into a past-life regression, and both of us hoping it would work. The woman leading the workshop guided us all into a simple regression and gave us time to silently explore whatever came up for us.

When it was time to share our experiences with the rest of the group, I was very timid about sharing my experience, which felt a little more substantial than pure imagination, but I had no idea if it was real.

I was a girl about nine years old living in Boston in the late 1700's. After running through the dining room to the stairway, I saw my mother standing on the balcony at the top of the stairs. She looked at me, started coughing, and fell all the way down the stairs, dying at my feet. I was shocked and didn't remember anything that happened after that.

While I shared my experience, my sweetie had listened quietly, her eyes getting wider the more I said. When I finished speaking, I asked her why she was looking at me the way she was. She shared her experience… She was a woman in her late thirties, standing on the balcony at the top of her stairs, looking down at her nine-year-old daughter at the bottom of the stairs. She tripped and feel down the stairs, dying near the bottom.

In sharing, my sweetie described in detail the dress she'd been wearing. It was the exact dress I'd seen on the woman at the top of the stairs but hadn't mentioned when I spoke. That whole experience was profound for both of us.

CHAPTER 32
SOUND HEALING

In some areas of our beings, sound supports energetic shifts much better than words, actions, or touch. It's especially beneficial for activating energies that support profound growth and for dissolving long held emotional challenges, long standing energy blockages, and deeply held beliefs. In addition to the simple technique I use, there's a modality called Music Therapy that's more structured and specific.

Here's the technique I use:
Before you make any sounds, discern where in your client's body or aura their energy is ready to be worked with. Do this by talking with your client about their challenges, gently laying your hands on different areas of their body, or slowly moving your hands through their aura. What you're listening or feeling for is a place in your client's being where something feels different – like it's oddly placed, a bit stuck, or calling for attention. When you find a place like that, believe your perception – this is where you'll begin working.

Begin making sounds as physically close as is practical to the area you identified in your client's body or aura. Continue making sounds until you feel the work is complete, allowing the intensity, tone, and location to change however it does through the process. Your client can make sounds with you or they can be silent. They can sit, stand, or lie down through the whole process or they can move their body as feels good to them. Follow your intuition and theirs when it comes to how long the sounds are used and what your client does while that's happening.

I prefer using sounds that I generate, or my client and I generate. This allows the tone and intensity to change with the needs of the moment and allows me to do this type of healing as the need arises. Some healers use recorded sounds or have other people at the session make sounds. Do whatever is most comfortable and practical for you.

Some ways to make sounds for healing:
- ♥ Singing, chanting, toning, or other vocal sounds
- ♥ Clapping hands
- ♥ Clicking fingers
- ♥ Stomping or tapping feet
- ♥ Using musical instruments such as drums, flutes, crystal bowls, Tibetan bells or bowls, rhythm sticks, ankle or wrist bells, etc.

CHAPTER 33
WORKING WITH SOULS & DREAMTIME HEALING

Facilitating healing for souls who aren't here on Earth is another aspect of being a healer. The impact of this type of work can be far reaching and the ripples can provide significant healing for people living here on Earth. Every healer who's intuitively open and enjoys working this way can do this. Time, space, who you are, who you're working with, the language you speak, and what type of healing is needed are not limitations for this form of healing. Working for the highest good of all is an essential foundation for this type of work.

The souls who ask for this type of healing may be living anywhere, at any time and in any form. Who they are and where they are doesn't matter. What matters is that they recognize an imbalance in their own being, they're seeking help with rebalancing, and you received their call for help. Receiving their call for help doesn't obligate you, it just means that you can help if you want to.

Although a financial exchange isn't part of doing this type of work, one of the gifts you will receive is unlearning centuries of human misconceptions. Among other things, it will help you understand how deeply connected all souls are, how simple it is to restore balance to any situation, how broad love is, and how fully safe we are in the amazing array of life.

Some basics:
- ♥ This work is energetic and spiritual – it's not physical actions on your part.
- ♥ You'll be working outside of time and space. This means distance doesn't matter and you can respond whenever you're ready to, even if that's quite some time before or after you receive the call for help.
- ♥ Sometimes these healing sessions will be completed in just a few seconds, sometimes they'll wander in and out of your awareness for days or weeks.
- ♥ You can stop participating in the healing anytime you want to. When you feel you've done all you can or are willing to, just stop. If the soul you've been working with wants more from you, politely refuse the invitation.
- ♥ You may find yourself spontaneously using wisdoms, techniques, or skills that are new to you or that were yours in another lifetime.
- ♥ You can choose to physically see, hear, or feel spirits. You can choose to be aware of them only through your thoughts. I choose thoughts because that helps me stay clear about whether I'm interacting with someone on the physical plane or someone in spirit.

Process for working with those on other planes:

1. When you feel someone's presence, calmly and lovingly ask what they need. It's important to ask what's needed, not what's wanted.

2. Now, notice the first thought that comes to your mind after you ask the question. Regardless of the nature of that first thought, it's that soul's way of describing the energy that will help them restore wholeness.

   > Souls sometimes ask for things that appear to us to be silly, odd, cruel, invasive, or dangerous. If you're uncomfortable with the request it's ok to decline the invitation to work with this soul. It's also ok to work with them and stay focused on the highest good of all. In these situations it can be helpful to remember that none of us know all that's needed for another soul to restore wholeness.

3. Now focus on your heart chakra and send the soul what they asked for.

4. When that feels complete, invite the them to come with you and return to the circle of love.

   > I prefer this to "sending them to the light" because I want the souls I work with to remember they're part of the whole and we're all part of the circle of love.

5. When that feels complete, thank the soul for returning to balance.

My Experience With This:

I receive intuitive calls for this type of healing when I'm sleeping and when I'm awake. If I don't have time to tend to it when I become aware of the request, I let the soul know I'll tend to it as soon as I have time. I've encountered a lot of different types of beings while doing this work and even though some have been very troubled when we first connected, all have been delightful and loving by the time we've completed our work together.

Some of My Favorite Stories About Working With Souls

While living in our sweet farm house that was over a century old, my partner and I noticed a woman coming into our room and sitting on the end of our bed some nights. We both felt the bed push downward a little when she sat down and because she was always very gentle and polite we just let her be. About six years after we'd first noticed her, we put the house up for sale and she stopped coming around at night. But the house wouldn't sell. Houses all around us were selling fast and a lot of people came through and loved our house and property, yet no one made an offer.

After many months of that, my partner and I walked through the whole house in meditation, trying to feel what could be stopping the sale. In a corner of the basement we felt the woman who liked to sit on our bed. Sitting near that corner and feeling into what we were perceiving, we realized she'd been attacked in the basement just a few years after the house was built. She felt safe with us and didn't want us to move out. Since that wasn't going to work for us, we looked into ways to heal her situation and that led us to putting sprigs of purple heather throughout the house for several days. The night we removed the heather, we felt her sit on the end of the bed again. One week later we sold the house.

During my first visit to my ancestral village in France, I felt the earth wrap gently around my feet every time I took a step. My mom was there too and described her experience as feeling like her feet were sinking into the ground. In this place, my direct ancestors had been born, lived, loved, and were lovingly laid to rest for many hundreds of years before my great-great-grandpa left in 1865. I heard their voices and felt their footprints under my feet as I walked the land. I felt their tears as their children died and their joy as children were born. I felt their hope and their fear as the local economy ebbed and flowed, as wars, famines, and diseases moved in and out of the area. I felt them welcome me; one they knew was their own. I knew I was loved by my ancestors and I belonged even though I could only stay for a few days.

I woke up in the middle of the night from a dream about a very angry man who identified himself as a fighter for a group that was violently sweeping across the Middle-East. He had participated in a terrorist attack the day before and had been killed during the attack. He stayed with me after I woke up and for several minutes I calmly listened to him rage about being dead and various other things. Then I told him I knew he'd come to me for healing. He quickly disagreed and disappeared. He showed up again the next afternoon and raged some more. Again, I calmly listened and then reminded him he'd come for healing. He left again. After several days and nights of these short interactions, he showed up one day and told me he was ready to heal.

Over the next few weeks we worked together to restore his wholeness and re-balance some of the destructive impacts he'd had on others. Then one day he asked what he could do in return for the help he'd received. I asked him to return to his people, the fighters and their families, and soften their hearts to the point where they could no longer tolerate doing the things they'd been doing. He agreed and during the next several weeks he came by for just a few brief visits.

Then one morning he showed up, clearly wanting my attention and very pleased with himself. He asked if I'd seen the news. I hadn't and he told me, "You have to look at the news." I immediately went to the daily news and the top article was about a group of two hundred people who'd been found on a bridge. They'd been captives of the group he'd been part of and were released during the night with no explanation as to why. When I asked if that was his doing, he beamed with pride and told me it was.

To this day, I'm awed and humbled to have experienced such profound evidence of how effective this type of healing can be.

Dreamtime Healing

This technique is more suited to your own sleeping hours than it is to session work with clients.

This can be used to address any situation you're inspired to help heal. Sometimes you'll be aware of things you can also do on the physical plane. Sometimes the dreamtime work is all that's needed. Sometimes it's all you'll be able to do and physical plane actions will be taken by others.

With clients who are also healers, or who are intuitively open, I sometimes explain how to do dreamtime healing and encourage them to use this technique to help heal things they're inspired to work with. Because this technique isn't conducive to time and space constraints, I don't use it in sessions. I do provide this support to clients when they show up in my dreams. For me, Dreamtime healing is pro-bono work; I never charge a fee for doing this.

If you prefer to sleep well while doing this work, it's beneficial to let those in spirit know you're available to do this type of healing only if it enhances your sleep and your overall well-being. Establish this agreement through a one-time meditation and deliver the message to whoever you connect with. Everyone else on the spirit plane will get the news and respect your side of the agreement.

Trust yourself to choose who you'll work with and what types of situations you're willing to participate in. You can define some of this ahead of time and let yourself sort out the rest of it in the moments when it matters. I can assure you, some of the healing opportunities that come your way will be so intriguing and so far beyond your imagination that you'll be inspired to work with them for the adventure and exploration of what's possible.

Dreamtime Healing Process

Give yourself permission to do healing work during your sleep, either in general or at specific times. Then when it's time for you to sleep, just sleep – if there's healing for you to do during your sleep it'll come to you. At times you'll work without ever knowing you've done it until someone tells you that you came to them in a dream and helped them with something. Sometimes you'll wake up during a dream and know that you're engaged in healing. You may also be awake and asleep intermittently. There will be times when you remember a lot of what you did. Other times you'll just have glimpses or you'll remember nothing. Always, your skill as a healer will grow through this work.

My Experience With This:

Early in my journey as a healer, I did a lot of my personal growth and spiritual exploration during my dreamtime. Even though I usually didn't remember my dreams, I often woke up in the morning with insights that were new to me.

I first became aware that I was working with others during my dreamtime after several people, over the course of many months, told me I'd helped them during a dream. I was fascinated by this and began waking up during some of those dreams. Of course, waking up refreshed in the morning became a bit challenging.

After a few months of not knowing how to sleep well without shutting it all off again, I told Spirit that I'm happy to do healing work in my dreamtime, for anyone anywhere in our universe or beyond, as long as it enhances my sleep and my well-being. From that night on I've slept very well while doing all sorts of work in my dreamtime, and consciously remembering a lot of it. Thirty-some years later, I still love doing this!

One of My Favorite Stories About Dreamtime Healing

Waking slightly during a dream, I found myself standing in the intersection between two corridors in a massive cathedral that reminded me of a medieval European church. An elderly man ran frantically toward me shouting, "I need help getting out!" I had no idea who he was or what was going on, but my heart was with him immediately and I knew I could help.

The corridor to my right had a huge stained glass window at the end of it so I motioned for him to follow me. As we ran down the corridor toward the window, I noticed how very tired he looked. Arriving at the window I pointed to a smaller side window and told him I could help him get out that way. He wasn't so sure, but took my hand anyway and let me support him as he climbed onto the window ledge. A lot of people stood in the courtyard below the window, though none of them appeared to notice us. I encouraged him to step out and fly upward, cautioning him not to jump downward into the people. He lifted his arms and quickly disappeared into the clouds. I returned to full sleep, thinking about that dream and wondering what it was all about.

When I woke up the next morning, the news had come out that the Pope died the night before. I felt spirit chills run down my spine and knew immediately the man in my dream had been his soul trying to find his way out of the Vatican. Just then I noticed his presence beside me so I asked him why he'd come to me; I wasn't Catholic or even Christian. He shrugged slightly and said he'd only been looking for someone who wasn't wishing he'd stay alive and when I responded, he was grateful for the help. Then he disappeared and I sat quietly for several minutes, awed at how easily we can find help whenever we need it.

SECTION 5

CONTEMPLATIONS & INSPIRATIONS

Wisdom is within me.

CHAPTER 34
CONTEMPLATIONS

Here are some things to think into deeply and discover your own truths in relation to them. Commonly held cultural perspectives can be contradictory to wisdom or can be lived in ways that contradict wisdom. They can encourage activities and beliefs that diminish long-term wholeness and fulfillment, or that expand or fulfill some while diminishing others. When considering things that can have deeply conflicting perspectives, please remember that feeling into your own heart and wisdom with the honesty of a neutral observer will bring your truths to conscious awareness.

Negative Thinking

Among many holistic teachers and healers, there's a bias toward positivity and away from negativity. Positivity is seen as beneficial to well-being and negativity is seen as detrimental. Teachings include the perspective that people who think negatively attract undesirable energies and situations, and they can spread that to the people around them.

This is another version of the "good vs. evil" perspective people use to justify abuse and keep humanity divided. All of the dichotomies of life on Earth walk hand-in-hand. Both aspects of each dichotomy, of each "oppositional" dynamic, support the well-being of all who live here. When we forget to live in wholeness, positive and negative can be equally harmful.

Karma

A lot of people believe karma is about punishment and rewards – that it's our penalty or blessing for things we've done in the past. Seeing karma this way supports the idea that we humans are unable to live our wholeness without an external incentive to help us do that.

My experience is that karma is a tool we use to help ourselves grow beyond the idea that being human gives us permission to be less than our wholeness. Whenever we want to, we can let go of karma and just choose to remember that being human expands our ability, right here right now, to be the unconditional love and wisdom we already are.

Soulmates

This term has come to mean partners in a romantic relationship that's meant to be; people who are so compelled to be in love that the relationship is inevitable and fulfilling in ways that no other love relationship has been or could be.

Our cultural perception tends to be that the level of attraction soulmates feel for each other means they're sexually attracted to one another. That perception can become an excuse to have an affair, to end a love relationship we're currently engaged in, or to put a lot of effort into making the soulmate relationship into a love relationship. None of these things are the foundations of a healthy love relationship; that alone is an indication the people involved misunderstand the reason for their connection.

I've observed that we have many soulmates during any given lifetime. We do feel a compelling draw to each other and our relationships are very fulfilling. Some of them are romantic and some aren't. Some last a long time and some don't. The purpose that's consistent in all of these relationships is that both souls are very committed to supporting each other in fulfilling their life purpose. The way each soulmate plays out that commitment is always their own to decide.

Indigo, Crystal, Rainbow, Millennial… Children and Adults
The widespread social consciousness and spiritual openness of these groups of people are obviously more expansive and inclusive than other recent generations in industrialized cultures. They've grown up in the midst of many adults who believe they'll be the generations who shift humanity out of destructiveness and into harmony. They're already showing us some of the wonderful ways they'll change the world, and some of the wounds they carry as a result of being human in this era. As wonderful as they are, and as much potential as they carry, why do we want our young people to have to save the world? Why are any of us willing to leave it to younger generations to clean up the messes we inherited and the ones we created? Why aren't we cleaning these things up ourselves so they don't have to?

Using Mind Altering Drugs to Expand Consciousness
Skilled guidance and aftercare are necessary for most people to fully integrate the spiritual benefits of hallucinogens such as ayahuasca, peyote, mushrooms, and similar plants and mixtures.

Our industrialized cultures don't have social structures in place that support full integration of drug aided spiritual experiences. We don't have councils of elders and seers who know us well and help us ground these experiences into the practical aspects of life. We may have a few people to support us for a few days after the drug experience, but they're typically not people who are part of our daily lives. They typically don't know us well enough to recognize when we're integrating the real wisdom of the experience and when we're getting lost in personal or cultural illusions.

If you choose to offer this to clients, please do so only if you're traditionally trained and working within the support structure of the culture your practices come from.

If you choose to use hallucinogens to expand your own consciousness, please do it with the guidance of people who have been traditionally trained and are offering you the experience within the context of the culture their practices come from and with the full support that culture provides.

Also, please be aware that using alcohol or other recreational drugs to expand consciousness gets convoluted for most people. For anyone who has used these recreationally or for comfort, their connection to them is reduced consciousness, not expanded consciousness. That contradiction of purpose tends to complicate the process of integrating spiritual awareness.

My perspective is that we humans need to remember and strengthen our ability to access our full consciousness using our own minds and body chemistry, without the use of external influences. Relying on external influences for this causes a lot of unnecessary confusion and effort in our own lives and the lives of others.

CHAPTER 35
INSPIRATIONS

These are some of my favorite stories about adventures I've had along my path as a healer. All of these are experiences that have expanded my awareness about how fully related we humans are to those in spirit, the Earth, and all others who live here.

Receiving Our New Home

My partner and I had sold our home and purchased a new one about one hundred miles away in the town she'd been transferred to. After the sale of our home, I was temporarily living with friends and anxiously waiting to get possession of our new home. One week before we were supposed to get possession, our realtor told us the seller hadn't found a new home and was backing out of the sale. We were beside ourselves.

That evening at a healing circle, we mentioned what had happened. After talking about the situation a bit, we all joined together in sending energy to the seller to help her find a house she absolutely loved and would be so excited about that she'd move before our possession date. Five days later our realtor told us she'd moved and we could pick up the keys for our new home.

Sky Helpers

While leading a healing ceremony for women who were sexual abuse survivors, we began the ceremony in full sunshine without a cloud in sight. After beginning our work outdoors around a fire, we entered a small lodge and closed ourselves in, immersing ourselves in complete darkness.

I passed a drum to the woman to my left and asked her to drum her heartbeat into our circle before speaking. She drummed, and we all heard thunder outside the lodge. The thunder stopped as soon as she started talking. Then she passed the drum to the woman to her left and when that woman drummed, thunder sounded again, and stopped again when she began talking. There were seventeen of us in the lodge, each speaking at intervals over the span of three hours, and the same thing happened each time one of us drummed and then spoke.

At some point rain suddenly began pouring outside the lodge and the rain stopped as soon as I declared the ceremony complete. When we stepped out of the lodge onto the rain soaked ground, the sun was again shining in a cloudless sky. We were all grateful and awed at the support we received from the sky beings.

Calling Love

A few years after my first marriage had ended I was finally ready for a new relationship. I'd already discovered that dating in my late 30's wasn't anywhere near as appealing as it had been in my teens and I didn't know how else to look for my new love. Sitting in my apartment on that cold February afternoon, I decided to do a ritual to invite her in. I didn't have much hope of success with that, but it did feel better than doing nothing.

So, I got up and started dancing. I danced for a long time, holding my invisible partner in my arms and imagining into the possibility that she would respond. And she did. I distinctly felt a hand reach through from the land of spirit and physically hold me hand. I kept dancing for awhile longer then ended my ritual full of laughter and hope.

Nothing else happened until many months later after I'd moved to another state. A few weeks after I started dating a woman there, I told her the story of my February ritual. With a very pleased look on her face, she told me about the ritual she did at about the same time, calling in her new love. We were both delighted and amazed at the similarity between our timing and the things we'd done in our rituals. And now we've been together for twenty-one years.

Grandpa Jemie

As I was digging deep into my family history I came across the name Jemie Dumas – one of my great-grandfathers from seven generations back. His name kind of bounced on my tongue when I said it aloud and I liked that so I kept saying it for a few days.

On one of those tongue bouncing days I was out in my garden picking green beans when I felt an invisible hand gently wrap around mine and stay there as I continued picking beans. After several minutes I felt a whisper of laughter and asked who was there. I felt his soft, clear response, "I'm your grandpa Jemie. It's been so long since I picked green beans! I love picking green beans!" I laughed with him and we continued picking beans and talking for about five more minutes.

Glacial Rock

After having some excavation done in my yard, I discovered a big glacial rock that had been dug up. It was in an inconvenient place for mowing so, as I was accustomed to doing with big rocks, I decided to move it to a flower bed. Based on size of the rock and distance of the move that looked to me to like it would be a pretty simple project.

When I tried to lift its edge to roll it, I discovered that rock had more density than any rock I'd ever moved. Of course I persisted and the rock resisted. After about thirty minutes of trying a variety of approaches, I finally sat on the ground and asked that beautiful pink quartzite rock to show me a way to move it the eighty-ish feet to the flower bed. No response.

So, I sat a little longer, wondering if I'd need to call my neighbor with a front end loader. Then I thought of one more way to try lifting the rock enough to start rolling it. That time I got that beautiful rock up on edge within a couple of minutes and rolled it all the way to the perfect place in the flower bed.

Squirrel Guide

During a group meditation in which we were learning to connect with Spirit Animals who are guides for us, I was really annoyed about a gray squirrel that kept chattering right outside a nearby open window. My mind kept wandering to the squirrel instead of staying focused on the guided meditation.

When the meditation ended, I listened to everyone else as they talked about the animals they'd connected with – jaguar, deer, eagle, python, wolf, giraffe and on and on. When it was my turn to talk, I told everyone I was really disappointed because I'd been so distracted by the squirrel's chatter that I hadn't been able to connect with any of my Spirit Animals.

After a short silence, the woman sitting next to me said she was disappointed because the deer that came to her stayed completely in spirit and the squirrel that came to me showed up in person. I thought she was joking until she mentioned that when she opened her eyes because of the squirrel's chatter, the squirrel was looking directly at me. And there it was, my big ah-ha for that day… the most ordinary beings in our everyday lives can be some of our wisest guides.

Luna/Jakunga

A couple of weeks after my beloved cat Luna died he told me he'd be back very soon and he'd come live with us again if we'd take him in. I wanted to believe our conversation was real, and Luna's return was do-able, and I was concerned that was just my wishful thinking. Luna patiently repeated his offer several times over the next few days. When I finally decided to set aside my resistance to being disappointed, I told him I'd be thrilled to have him come live with us again whenever he was ready to.

As our conversation continued over the next few months, Luna told me he'd return home in July. He shared a lot of fascinating things about the process of deciding his purpose for the coming lifetime, finding his new parents, and connecting with his new body. While I took all of that in, I became increasingly concerned about our ability to find each other again. With him in a different body, being born who knows where, and me blindly trying to recognize him even if he was right in front of my eyes, I had more than a few visions of ending up with dozens of kittens in my effort to make sure I found him.

In his gently pragmatic way, Luna reminded me everything would be fine and figuring out the logistics of finding each other was his job, just like it had been the first time he found me. To reassure me a bit, he gave me signs to look for; very recognizable things he'd do when we met so I'd know it was him.

In late June I started searching area animal shelters for kittens who'd be the right age in July. After many days of no luck, I stopped searching and asked Luna to make sure he got to me safely. A few days later, I felt his excited presence. He said, "I'm here!" As I sat talking with him, I looked all around the garden trying to see where he was.

He let me look for awhile before laughing and telling me to go inside and call the local shelter. Having looked at the shelter's website a few hours earlier, I knew there were no kittens available for adoption. I told him that and he said, "Yes there are. I'm here!"

So I looked at the shelter's still kitten-less website again and then called to put my name on a waiting list. Much to my surprise, they told me a litter of kittens the right age had arrived a few days earlier. They weren't ready for adoption yet, but I could meet them that day. My wife and I were at the shelter as soon as the doors opened. Within minutes of meeting the babies, one of the boys had shown us every sign Luna told me to look for. Knowing we'd found our boy, we signed the paperwork and headed home to wait for the day he could go home with us.

Later that day I was trying to figure out a name for our new little one when Luna popped in and declared, "I am Jakunga!" He spelled the name for me and I teased him about that being a really powerful name for such a little guy, to which he just responded, "I am Jakunga!", laughed at me, and disappeared. Having never heard the word before, I checked online and found only one reference to Jakunga. It's used in a role-playing game as the name of something Earth's moon aligns with once every thousand years and when the alignment occurs, magical things happen. I laughed for quite awhile about that one!

A few weeks later we brought Jakunga home. Watching him settle in during his first few weeks with us was hilarious, heart-warming, and just plain amazing. He's different than Luna and exactly like him at the same time. I'm awestruck that, during one of my own lifetimes, I get to know this beautiful soul through two of his.

SECTION 6

SELF-GUIDED HEALING TECHNIQUES

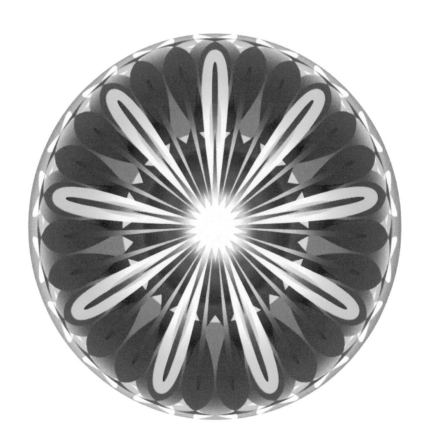

I'm the one I've been waiting for.

Most people are capable of creating and sustaining their own wholeness and I feel it's important for each person to regain their full personal power with this. When any of the techniques in this section will benefit a client, I encourage you to ask them to expand on what you do together by also doing some healing on their own.

You have my permission to copy and share pages 184 thru 205.

EXPANDING YOUR PERSPECTIVE

Growing Beyond Limitations

This is used to move beyond self-limiting decisions, beliefs, and perspectives you're no longer experiencing as beneficial.

Growing Beyond Limitations Process:

Do this with your eyes closed or open, whichever feels best to you.

1. Take a few gentle deep breaths and bring yourself to center.
2. Now hold your hands together out in front of you, palms up, forming an open basket.
3. Imagine your hands filling up with all the things you use to limit yourself or your experience of life. Whatever those things are, lovingly lay each of them into your palm basket.
4. Now imagine a beautiful basket sitting on the floor at your feet. Choosing one thing at a time from among the things you're holding in your hands, lovingly fill the beautiful basket at your feet with each limitation you want to keep.
5. Now appreciate and thank all of the limitations that are still in your palm basket for the ways they supported you in the past.
6. Now, raise your palm basket up toward the sky and give permission for all the things that remain there to return to the universe and make themselves available to the next person who can benefit from their help.
7. Now be with yourself for a minute or so and fill your heart with gratitude and love for all the tools you use to support yourself in being you.

Growing Beyond Paradigms

This is used to release yourself from participating in imbalances that undermine well-being for you or others. Some examples of this include seeing others as inferior, living in fear, creating personal gain at the expense of others, damaging Earth's natural environment, being abusive, ignoring free will, seeking rescue, participating in addictions, etc.

Expect that during the first few weeks after doing this type of healing you'll encounter many opportunities to change your mind. It may feel like you're being presented with everything that enticed you to participate in the paradigm you chose to grow beyond. This happens because you're engaged in a healing process that has profound impacts beyond your own life. You're asking yourself to fully commit to this new way of being, regardless of any invitations to step back into things that support what you chose to grow beyond.

Growing Beyond Paradigms process:

1. Sit in meditation and breathe gently until you feel centered and connected with your concept of Spirit. Then tell Spirit something to this effect: I'm ready to completely release all aspects of (…your chosen paradigm) from every part of my being. I have no idea how to do this. Please show me the kindest, gentlest way.
2. Sit quietly for another few minutes and then go on about your day. You may receive some guidance during your meditation. Most of your guidance will come to you in the lived moments that will create this change.

Wisdom Reading

This is used to support clarity during times of stress or confusion and to grow into new ways of thinking. You'll need a deck of divinations cards and a book that gives the meaning of each card. Tarot or some other type of divination deck will work well.

1. Focus on a simple question such as, "What's here for me to know today?"
2. Shuffle your deck or mix the cards up in some other way.
3. Draw three cards at random and look at the cards.
4. Using the book that goes with your deck, read the definition of each card and make note of anything that stands out to you while reading.
5. Sit for a few minutes with whatever came up for you while reading.
6. Then give your mind permission to keep working with this information while you go on about your day.

Thought For The Day

This is a process that helps you see the bigger picture, find your own wisdom, and engage your creative thinking. It frees your mind to connect the dots and generate conscious insight into anything you want to explore.

Choose one situation that you find to be challenging or that you want to explore. This can be anything from the most personal and private concern all the way to a widely known global concern. If several things come up, make a list and work with them one at a time.

Now form a question or short sentence that addresses what you want to explore. Give your mind permission to continue thinking about that as you go through the rest of your day. Don't put any additional effort into this – just let it be in the back of your mind for the day. The thought may periodically come to the surface and then return to the background. At some point, that day or another, you'll consciously understand the information you were seeking.

Examples:
The exploration: lack of motivation.
The question: "If I knew what motivates me, what do I imagine that to be?"

The exploration: challenges with physical health.
The question: "What does my body need from me right now?"

The exploration: human cruelty.
The question: "What can I do to expand human kindness?"

PHYSICAL ACTIVITY

Active Meditation

This is used for the same reasons as all other forms of meditation, it's just done while engaging in a physical activity. This is especially beneficial when you have a hard time staying focused during still meditations and when you want to be consciously spiritually engaged and well-grounded at the same time.

Choose a physical activity that doesn't require your full attention. Activities that work well are ones that keep your body busy, your mind engaged most of the time, and allow space for your mind to wander without stopping the physical activity. Some activities that work well include: gardening, painting a large area, walking, running, washing dishes, mowing grass, etc.

When you have a good start on the activity, give your mind a focus that you're curious about and let your thoughts run in the background while you continue with what you're doing. From time to time those thoughts will naturally come to your attention, then return to the background.

Trust yourself to consciously remember anything that really matters. Don't work at this, just trust. If you work to remember the thoughts that come with this type of meditation, you'll stop the meditative process and, along with the information you actually desire, you'll remember a confusing mix of things that are just information processing.

Body/Mind Alignment

This is done to help your body align with healing, growth, and change. This can be particularly helpful when your thinking becomes rigid or stuck, when you lack confidence, or you're resisting a shift you want to make.

The process is free flowing and creative – there's no right or wrong way to do this, there's only your way. If music makes this more interesting, inspiring, or fun for you, include it in what you're doing.

Begin by focusing on what you want to live into and then start moving however you want to in the moment. Continue moving any way your mind or body want to, following your inspirations until you feel full and complete.

Rage Release

When your emotions go to the point of rage, intense anger, intense frustration, or when any of those things show up out of proportion to a current experience, you're living with built-up rage. This process is used to release that old rage so you can respond to current situations based on what's occurring in the present.

Plan on about one hour of uninterrupted time for this. In addition to releasing rage, this healing process is designed to help you learn that you can responsibly release this intense emotion without the help of others. If you feel the need to have someone with you during this time, choose someone you trust who agrees to maintain your privacy and to be a calming, supportive ally if that's needed. This person shouldn't be afraid of rage and should be someone who can help you restore balance if you feel your emotions are too intense for you to handle.

Rage Release Process:

This is best done when you're completely alone and won't be seen or heard by others. Choose a place where you can be alone for at least one hour with no interruptions and no human witnesses.

1. After taking a few gentle deep breaths, begin expressing some emotions. If your emotions feel blocked, it can be helpful to begin by laughing until your more challenging emotions start to emerge.
2. Express any emotions that come up. Yell, swear, sing, laugh, scream, cry, dance, roll on the ground, stomp around… With the exception of physical violence or destruction of objects, physically express whatever comes up for you. Do this through your voice and your body movements.
3. Stay with this for at least fifteen minutes and continue longer if that feels right to you.
4. If you become concerned about the intensity of your emotions, or you feel you're about to become violent, pause for a few minutes, sit quietly, and take some gentle slow breaths before continuing your release process. The goal is to release your pain from old wounds without creating new situations you'll have to correct or apologize for.
5. Stay with this process until all you can do is laugh about how absurd it would look if someone saw you doing this. You may find that it's beneficial to repeat this process periodically.
6. When you feel complete with this wild dance with your emotions, take a little time to be tender, loving, and kind to yourself. Eat something you enjoy, wrap yourself in a long hug, sing yourself a love song, take a nap. Do whatever gentleness toward yourself feels good to you.

Body Pendulum

This is used to discern your own wisdom whenever you want to.

To get clear answers, ask individual yes/no questions. If you tend to include more than one question in a statement, separate them into individual questions and ask each one separately. A multiple question looks like this: Is it time for me to find a new job or should I stay with my current employer?

When doing this, "yes" means yes; "no" means no; "maybe" means the question isn't completely clear or there are variables that make the answer uncertain.

Body Pendulum Process:

1. Sit or stand in a way that allows your body to sway slightly.
2. Gently lay your hand on your solar-plexus chakra and keep your focus there.
3. Now take a gentle deep breath and ask your body to show you a "yes". Pay attention to your body's response.
4. Now take a gentle deep breath and ask your body to show you a "no". Pay attention to your body's response.
5. Now take a gentle deep breath and ask your body to show you a "maybe" Pay attention to your body's response.
6. Now take a gentle deep breath, ask a clear yes or no question and pay attention to your body's response.

PHYSICAL HEALTH & WELL-BEING

Chakra Balancing

This is used to support your well-being on all levels. Chakras are energy centers in your body that support your ability to live a vibrant, healthy, fulfilling life. If you're feeling out of balance in any way, balancing one or more of your chakras can be beneficial.

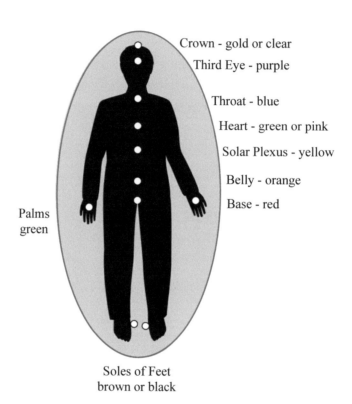

Crown - gold or clear

Third Eye - purple

Throat - blue

Heart - green or pink

Solar Plexus - yellow

Belly - orange

Base - red

Palms
green

Soles of Feet
brown or black

Some Ways to Balance Your Chakras:

Sit quietly for a few minutes, holding the intention of balancing or clearing the energy of one or more chakras. When you feel ready, do one of these things:

- ♥ Smudge the chakra with sage.
- ♥ On the chakra, lay a stone that feels right to you.
- ♥ Slowly move your palms over the chakra in a circular motion, clockwise or counterclockwise, whichever direction feels right to you.
- ♥ Fill the chakra with its native color either by visualization or by laying an object of the appropriate color on the chakra.
- ♥ Hold a piece of the stone kyanite in your hand or lay it on the chakra.

- ♥ Gently touch the tips of your thumbs and fingers to the tips of your toes and keep them there for a few minutes. Do this with all fingers and toes at the same, touching your thumbs to your big toes, index fingers to second toes, middle to middle, ring to fourth, and little fingers to little toes.

Lymph System Drain

This is done to strengthen your immune system, relieve allergies, and heal viral and bacterial infections.

Process for Lymph System Drain

1. Massage the soles of both feet.
2. Using your fingertips, stimulate the points in the web between each of your fingers and toes.
3. Using your fingertips, stimulate your liver and kidneys by pressing the points on the outside of each calf and thigh.
4. Press your knuckle firmly into each sciatic point and release when the discomfort in the point subsides.
5. Press your knuckle firmly into each rear hip point and release when the discomfort in the point subsides.
6. Using your knuckle, stimulate the points along both sides of your spine by pressing approximately every two inches from the top of your hips to the base of your neck.
7. Using your fingertips, stimulate the points on each shoulder blade. When working on yourself this can be difficult – just do the best you can.
8. Using your fingertips, gently stimulate the lymph nodes at your pelvis by pressing on them.
9. Using your fingertips, stimulate your front hip points by pressing on them.
10. Using your fingertips, rake your back on each side, moving along the rib cage, from your spine to the front of your sides.
11. Massage around your breasts using a kneading motion and working from all directions.
12. Firmly squeeze under each arm pit three or four times.
13. Using your fingertips, pump the points below your collar bones and shoulder joints.
14. Using your fingertips, stimulate the points along the top of your collar bones by pressing approximately every inch from your shoulder to the center of your collar bones.
15. Using your hands, massage down from your collar bones to your belly using long deep strokes.
16. Using your hands, do a Sun/Moon massage on your belly.

    Starting at the top of your right hip, push down and massage the colon in a circular motion moving from your right hip up to the bottom of your ribs on the right, then across toward your ribs on the left and down to your left hip. Then massage down to the top of your pelvis and across the top of your pelvic bone up toward your right hip. Repeat this several times, working as deeply as is comfortable for your body.

17. Firmly squeeze each shoulder from the top.
18. Firmly squeeze the lymph nodes under your chin.

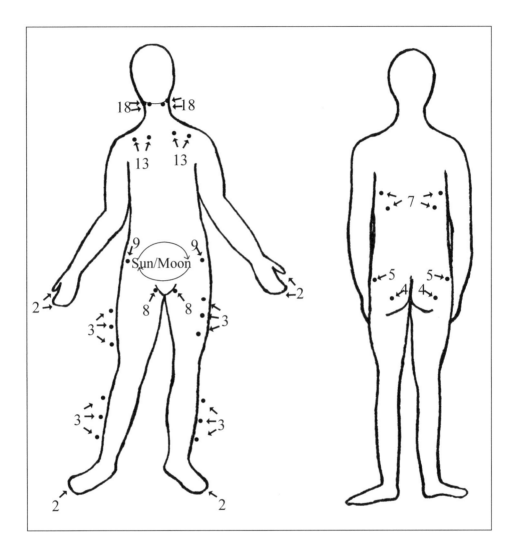

RELATIONSHIPS WITH OTHERS

Acknowledgements

This process helps couples stay aware of what each other does to support their relationship. It helps each of you know what the other sees you doing and gives each of you an opportunity to name the things you do that your beloved may have overlooked or misunderstood.

Plan on 15 - 20 minutes of uninterrupted time during which you focus completely on each other.

Do this once weekly for as long as it feels right to both of you. After that, do this periodically to help you stay present to each other's love and appreciation.

Acknowledgements Process:

Sit facing each other, preferably on comfortable seating that allows you to touch each other. Decide who will speak first and who will listen first. Do the process all the way through, then switch roles and do it all the way through again.

♥ When speaking:

1. One thing at a time, tell your beloved all the things you see her/him doing to support your love and your life together. Before each item, say, "I acknowledge you for…".

     Examples: going to work each day, enjoying my mom, making our home comfortable, being so creative…

2. When you're done speaking, ask your beloved if she/he received these acknowledgements.

3. If the answer is "no", ask your beloved if she/he would like you to repeat anything or would like a moment to soak them in.

4. When your beloved says they've received your acknowledgements, ask if there's anything more they'd like to be acknowledged for.

5. If the answer is "yes", simply acknowledge them for whatever else they say they want. Don't question or judge anything and don't ask for an explanation. Just acknowledge them.

6. When this is complete, switch roles.

♥ When listening:

1. Listen silently and let yourself absorb what your beloved says. Don't comment or ask for explanations. Just receive. These are the things your beloved notices as acts of love, kindness, or support.

2. When your beloved asks you if you want to be acknowledged for anything else, it's your time to tell your beloved the acts of love, kindness, or support you do and they may not be noticing as gifts

of love. Name those things one at a time, pausing between each to give your beloved time to acknowledge you.

♥ After both of you have spoken and listened, finish with a warm hug and "I love you."

Cord Release

This is used to support you with disengaging from relationship dynamics that are diminishing your well-being and to finish disengaging from relationships that have ended.

Cord Release Process:

1. Close your eyes and breathe gently, bringing yourself to center.
2. Ask your (…sister, mom, spouse, ex, son, etc.…) to come join you and sit about six inches away facing you, mirroring your body posture without touching you.
3. Now take a gentle deep breath and feel into the area between your bodies. You'll notice cords of two different colors there, running from your body to hers/his. The cords of one color belong to you and the other to her/him.
4. Now run your hand downward between your bodies, gently disconnecting her/his cords from your body, sliding them back over to her/him. If she/he tries to reconnect any of the cords, gently give them back again.
5. Now run your hand downward between your bodies again, and gently disconnect your cords from her/his body, bringing them back to you and laying them in your lap. Now let them gently dissolve into your body.
6. Now take a gentle deep breath, and again feel into the area between your bodies. If you find more cords, repeat steps 4, 5, and 6 again. When you don't find anymore cords, go to step 7.
7. Now thank her/him for being here and watch as she/he moves away and disappears completely.
8. Sit quietly for a few minutes and then go on about your day.

Releasing Teachers

This is done to help yourself live beyond embedded lessons that no longer support your well-being. Your teachers for these lessons may be people, animals, experiences, life circumstance, or anything else outside of yourself. It's helpful to name those teachers whatever you call them… Mom, Jack, poverty, ADHD, sunlight, poison ivy, depression, cancer, etc.

Releasing Teachers Process:

1. Close your eyes and take a few gentle breaths, bringing yourself to center.
2. Now invite (…name you call your chosen teacher) to come sit with you as your honored guest.
3. Now thank (… your chosen teacher) for all that you've learned from her/him.
4. Now tell (… your chosen teacher) that you'll be our own teacher from here forward and she/he is released from all responsibility to teach you anything more. She/he is now free to share their wisdom with whoever will benefit from it next.
5. Now watch quietly while she/he moves away from you and disappears.

Speaking With Deceased Loved Ones

This is done to help heal your grief about loved ones who've died and to transform your relationships with them into forms that support your ability to thrive in your life. Please know that it's normal for loved ones to be close around during the first several days or weeks after their death and then be unavailable for several months before being available again.

Here's a way to do this:
1. Sit quietly and invite your loved one to join you.
2. Continue sitting quietly for another minute or two.
3. Then, whether or not you feel their presence, begin your conversation with them either by speaking out loud or with your mind,. Tell your loved one whatever is on your mind or heart. Let your emotions be whatever they are while you're speaking.
4. When you've finished speaking, sit quietly for at least fifteen minutes and just receive whatever comes back to you. Don't look for specific things to happen, just notice what does happen, however subtle or obvious it is.
5. When you feel complete with your visit, or you feel the energy around you go quiet or empty, thank your loved one and then go on about your day.

RELATIONSHIP WITH YOURSELF

Affirmations

Affirmations are used to help you live into a new way of being. Saying your affirmations out loud gets your whole body engaged in the process, which makes it much easier to live the changes you want to make.

Wording your affirmations in the present tense helps you make them lived experiences quickly rather than keeping the shift in the future. Wording them to describe the end result you want helps you make the changes you seek. Wording affirmations to focus on eliminating something you don't want keeps you focused on what you don't want. Wording them too specifically eliminates a lot of wonderful options you haven't thought of yet.

Here are some examples of what I'm talking about:
~ Elimination wording: I'm done with this unsatisfying job.
~ Future wording: I'll get a job that's fully satisfying to me.
~ Specific wording: I have the job I applied for with Proctor.
~ Wording that's focused on the end result, present tense, and open to new possibilities: I have a job that's fully satisfying to me.

Self-Love

This is done to help you fully love and embrace yourself. When you fully love and embrace yourself, your capacity and skill for loving others will be fully available to you. You may feel awkward, self-conscious, undeserving, or in some other way uncomfortable when you first begin doing this. You may think you're lying to yourself. Those feelings are an indication of your deep need to love and embrace yourself.

Repeat this process daily until it becomes an experience that makes your heart sing. When that time comes, you're loving you well. After that, continue doing this daily if you want to, or do it again as needed or desired.

Self-Love Process:
1. Stand in front of a mirror and look directly into your own eyes. Speaking out loud, tell yourself, "I love you absolutely and unconditionally. You are the most precious person to me."
2. Hold your eye contact for a few minutes allowing your emotions to flow as needed.
3. When you feel complete with this, go on about your day.

Body Memory Healing

This is used to heal trauma or painful memories that you've stored in your body. These memories may have come from physical injuries, emotional challenges, or intense stress.

Give yourself at least 45 minutes of quiet, uninterrupted time to do this healing process. If you'd like, play some recorded music at a volume that's soothing to you. Get into a relaxed position that you'll be comfortable with for however long you're working with this.

If you feel resistance at any time during this healing process, pause and shift position a bit, gently breathe for a few seconds. and then continue.

1. Close your eyes and take three or four deep gentle breaths.
2. Beginning with the top of your head, mentally check in with each area of your body. Pause for a few seconds and notice your scalp, your forehead and face, then the back of your neck, then your throat.
3. Continue moving your attention down your body, pausing and noticing each area all the way out to your fingertips and down to the tips of your toes and the soles of your feet.
4. Pause and breathe gently for a few seconds.
5. Stay relaxed and notice your body's sensations. Begin gently moving any area of your body that you feel drawn to.
6. For at least another fifteen minutes, continue lovingly changing positions and moving in any ways that feel good to you. Pause when you want to, relaxing into the position you're in at the time. Then move again in any ways that feel good to you. If emotions come up while you're doing this, allow them to flow while you continue moving and pausing.
7. When you feel complete with this, pause and breathe gently for a little bit. Then drink a glass of water and sit quietly until you feel fully present.

Childhood Grief Healing

This is done to heal the wounds of childhood and the ways they've impacted your adult years. I suggest doing this when you can be completely alone so you can fully express whatever comes up with no concern about being observed or heard by others. Do this where you can sit comfortably. It's beneficial to have tissues handy and water to drink throughout this process. Plan on about 45 minutes for this.

Childhood Grief Healing Process:

1. Face the East and breathe gently, bringing yourself to center.
2. Focus on your life from birth to age 12 and explore what's there – any memories or lack of them, emotions, thoughts, fears, happy times, etc.
3. Now start laughing. Fake the laughter if it doesn't come naturally. Keep laughing even if it feels disconnected from that part of your life.
4. Continue laughing, allowing your laughter to shift into words and other emotions as they come up.
5. When you feel complete with this, pause and sit quietly for a minute or so.
6. Now face the South and breathe gently, bringing yourself to center.
7. Focus on your life from age 12 to age 19 and explore what's there.
8. Repeat steps 3, 4, and 5.
9. Now face the West and breathe gently, bringing yourself to center.
10. Focus on the first half of your adult life and explore what's there.
11. Repeat steps 3, 4, and 5.
12. Now face the North and breathe gently, bringing yourself to center.
13. Focus on the second half of your adult life and explore what's there.
14. Repeat steps 3, 4, and 5.
15. Now sit in the center of the area you've been working in and explore what you want for your future.
16. Now do something to get your body involved – stand up and dance or move around, stay seated and clap your hands or tap your feet, sing, tone, chant, play a drum, etc.
17. Continue letting your body and mind play with your future until you feel full, a bit inspired, and complete with this process.
18. Sit quietly and breathe gently for at least a few minutes and let it all settle in before you go on about your day.

Expanding Self-Trust

This is used to help you regain your center when you feel stressed, intimidated, overwhelmed, or endangered by a challenge you're facing. After you've done this a few times, you'll be able to do it in a matter of seconds and while you're in the midst of challenging situations.

Expanding Self-Trust Process:

1. Sitting quietly, take a few gentle deep breaths and bringing yourself to center.
2. Now focus on your solar-plexus chakra, breathe gently, and imagine the color yellow filling that chakra.
3. Now gently expand the yellow through your entire body and out into your aura. Breathe there for several seconds.
4. Now gently expand the yellow out as far as you can get it and then a little farther. Take it out far enough that you're bigger than any challenge you could ever face.
5. Now breathe gently and stay in this expanded yellow energy until you feel overflowing with it.
6. Now gently relax and allow the yellow to come all the way back into your solar-plexus chakra. Rest there for a few minutes before going on about your day.

Future-Self Guidance

Future-Self Guidance is used to support your ability to fully live changes you want to make in your life or your way of being. This is especially effective for making changes you think you don't know how to make, you're afraid to make, or you believe are impossible or unattainable.

Your future-selves will come at your request. They're invested in you living the future they represent and they're happy to reach back in time and provide the roadmap to it. A future-self typically won't give any guidance during meditation. The guidance will come in the moments when you're engaged in something that will either bring you closer to this future or take you further away from it.

You're most likely to notice this healing playing out in your life by gradually noticing you're effortlessly making decisions that support the future you want to live. This is a very gentle, natural shift in decision making. It comes from within and generally occurs without you focusing on changing your behavior.

The focus can be on any aspect of your life, big or small. It's important for you to word your own description of the future-self you want to receive guidance from so the description fits you perfectly. Here are some suggestions for you to consider putting into your own words:

- ♥ My future-self who is completely delighted with all aspects of her/his life.
- ♥ My future-self who is financially secure.
- ♥ My future-self who has completely healed from PTSD.
- ♥ My future-self who has successfully raised my children.
- ♥ My future-self who has grown beyond the need for any form of addiction.

Future-Self Guidance Process

Focus on one future-self at a time. It's fine to work with multiple future-selves concurrently. To give your body time to align well with each future-self, initiate each connection in separate meditations that are at least 24 hours apart.

1. Name the future-self you want to work with as clearly as you can.
2. Close your eyes and breathe gently, bringing yourself to center.
3. When you feel ready, invite the future-self you named to come sit with you.
4. Sit quietly for a few minutes and just feel into the energy around you.
5. Now, whether or not you feel the presence of this future-self, ask her/him, "Please guide every action I take and every decision I make to insure that yours is the reality I live."
6. Sit quietly for a few minutes, then thank her/him for helping you.
7. When you're ready, open your eyes and go on about your day.

Recognizing Right Timing

This is done to create ease and flow in your life.

Here are some ways to do this:

♥ With your body, feel your energy and emotions about the situation you're focused on. If you feel wide open and relaxed, the time is right. If you feel hesitant or like you'll have to protect yourself, convince someone, push, or force something, these are indications it's not the right time.

♥ When you feel completely inspired to do or say something that impacts only you, go for it. If you feel any resistance, assume the resistance is there because it's helping you grow.

♥ Use your body as a pendulum.

Higher-Self Guidance

This process is done to help you develop immediate access to your highest wisdom in all situations. Repeat this process periodically until it's easy for you to access your wisdom whenever you want to. Your higher-self is the part of your soul that lives outside of your human self and can see the bigger picture in all situations.

Higher-Self Guidance Process:

1. Sit quietly, take a few gentle breaths, and bring yourself to center.
2. Now ask your higher-self to come sit with you.
3. Sit quietly for a few seconds and notice what's going on around you. You may feel a shift in the energy around you, you may not.
4. When you feel ready, talk with your higher-self like you'd talk with a trusted, wise advisor. Ask questions, talk about your confusion, talk about things that are bothering you or things you'd like to be able to do.
5. When you feel like you've said all that's in your heart for now, sit quietly for at least fifteen minutes and notice what comes back to you. You may find words in your mind, you may feel comforted or loved, you may feel alone. It's all ok. Just absorb whatever is there without judging it as real or unreal, good or bad, helpful or not.
6. When you feel complete with this, thank your higher-self for joining you and then go on about your day.

SLEEPTIME HEALING

Sensory Clearing

It's most effective to do this process just before you'll be sleeping for several hours. This allows the process to continue gently unfolding while you sleep.

Sensory Clearing is used to clear body memories after an intimate relationship ends, after the death of a loved one, when an addiction is being released, and after physical, mental, or emotional trauma. It's also beneficial to do this at least once a year to help maintain overall well-being by clearing body memories of experiences that have fulfilled their purpose or are insignificant (ie: seeing a neighbor's dog wander through the yard).

When doing a Sensory Clearing, it's important to work with only one sense on any given day. It's also best to clear all five senses over a short period of time.

For sound, work with your ears, mouth and bones. For touch, work with your skin, muscles and bones. For taste, work with your mouth and tongue. For smell, work with your nose. For sight, work with your eyes.

I've used "sight" as the example in the process description.

Sensory Clearing Process:
Set aside 45 minutes during which you won't be disturbed. If you it feels good to you, put on a recording of soft music without identifiable words.

1. Lie down where you'll be comfortable staying in pretty much the same position for about thirty minutes.
2. Close your eyes and keep them closed for the entire process.
3. Give your eyes permission to release all visual memories that no longer support your growth or happiness.
4. Relax and allow whatever floats across your vision to just pass through. From time to time affirm that each thing you see is being released. Some of your visual memories may be pleasant, some unpleasant, and some may have no emotional charge at all. It doesn't matter. Trust your own wisdom and know that your body will give you only memories that you no longer need to hold. Also trust your body to give you all the visual memories that are ready to be released today.
5. Stay with this for as long as the visuals come.
6. When they stop, relax quietly for a few minutes and then drift into sleep or gently return to your ordinary activities.

Sensory Connection

It's most effective to do this process just before you'll be sleeping for several hours. This allows the process to continue gently unfolding while you sleep.

Sensory Connection is used to heal disconnections between your mind and body. When done after the complete series of Sensory Clearings it's very beneficial for people who've experienced physical violence, serious illness or injury, or who have PTSD. It's also beneficial for healing the phantom aspects of paralysis or amputation and can help relieve some neurological challenges.

Sensory Connection Process:

While lying comfortably in your bed…

1. Hold your hands gently over your ears, and imagine a bridge between each ear and your brain. Expand that bridge into an energy field that includes your ears, your brain, and the wisdom of your soul.
2. Hold your hands gently over your eyes, and imagine a bridge between each eye and your brain. Expand that bridge into an energy field that includes your eyes, your brain, and the wisdom of your soul.
3. Touch your nose, and imagine a bridge between your nose and your brain. Expand that bridge into an energy field that includes your nose, your brain, and the wisdom of your soul.
4. Touch your tongue, and imagine a bridge between your tongue and your brain. Expand that bridge into an energy field that includes your tongue, your brain, and the wisdom of your soul.
5. Run your hands over your skin, and imagine a bridge between your skin and your brain. Expand that bridge into an energy field that includes all of your skin, your brain, and the wisdom of your soul.
6. Imagine all of your sensory organs simultaneously and picture them as interconnected aspects of your whole being. Lay quietly for several minutes until you feel complete with this.

Past-Life Completion

Past-life completion is used to heal dynamics that are rooted in your past-lives and are causing undesirable challenges in your current lifetime.

Before you begin this process you'll need to have at least a little information about the lifetime that's ready to be completed. That information can come through your own discernment process or you can receive it from someone else. If multiple lifetimes are ready for completion, please do this process separately for each lifetime, allowing at least 24 hours between them.

Past-Life Completion Process:

1. When you're ready to sleep for at least five or six hours, lay quietly in bed and take a few minutes to remember what you can of the information you received about the lifetime you're ready to complete. Trust that what you remember is all that's important for the completion process.
2. Then give your mind permission to remember anything else you need to know about the lifetime and lay quietly for several more minutes. You may or may not remember anything else.
3. When you're satisfied that you've received all the information that's going to come, state this intention, "While I'm sleeping I'll gracefully and gently finish all unfinished business from this lifetime."
4. Then go to sleep. By the time you wake up the the residual energies of the lifetime will be completed.

APPENDIX A
HOLISTIC HEALING METHODS

From the wide array of holistic healing methods, this is a summary of the ones I'm most familiar with and most enjoy using. Details about how to work with some of these are in this book.

Affirmations

> Uses: All layers of healing. Can be done in person or long distance. Recipient must repeatedly write, say, read, or listen to affirmations. Affirmations only work if the recipient's mind actively participates in the process.

Ancestral

> Uses: All layers of healing. Especially beneficial for spiritual, emotional, & mental healing. Family healing: requires participation of at least one family member. Human-wide healing: can be done in groups or by one person. Can be in person or long distance.

Animal Communication

> Uses: All layers of healing for the animal. Also beneficial for healing relationships between animals and people. Can be done with the animal alone or with the animal and its people together. Can be done in person or long distance.

Art

> Uses: All layers of healing. Sometimes this is passive observation, sometimes the recipient actively participates. Methods that don't include physical participation are usually less effective with physical healing than other holistic methods are. Can be done in person or long distance.

Body Wisdom

> Uses: All layers of healing. Especially beneficial for mental, physical and emotional healing. Requires the recipient's active participation. Can be done in person or long distance.

Bodywork

> Uses: All layers of healing. This includes Acupressure, Massage, Polarity, Qigong, Rolfing and similar techniques. Some techniques are beneficial for animals. Always done in person.

Channeling

> Uses: All layers of healing. Especially beneficial for spiritual, emotional, and mental healing. Can be beneficial for any being and all species. Can be done in person or long distance.

Color

    Uses: All layers of healing. Beneficial for most types of beings. Most effective when done in person, can be done long distance.

Dreamtime

    Uses: All layers of healing. Best done long distance.

Energywork

    Uses: All layers of healing. Can be beneficial for any type of being and all species. Can be done in person or long distance.

Essential Oils

    Uses: All layers of healing. Can be used with humans and animals. Some species and individuals will have adverse reactions to some oils. Requires the recipient to use oils as suggested. Can be done in person or long distance.

Flower Essences

    Uses: All layers of healing. Especially beneficial for spiritual, mental, and emotional healing. Requires the recipient to use each essence as suggested. Can be done in person or long distance.

Future-Self

    Uses: All layers of healing. Requires the recipient's active mental participation. Can be done in person or long distance.

Guided Meditation

    Uses: All layers of healing. Especially beneficial for emotional, mental and spiritual healing and growth. Can be done in person of long distance.

Hands-on-Healing

    Uses: All layers of healing. Especially beneficial for emotional and physical healing. Can be done with animals. Always done in-person.

Herbs

    Uses: Physical and emotional healing. Requires the recipient to use the herbs as suggested. Can be done in person or long distance.

Karmic

    Uses: All layers of healing. Especially beneficial for spiritual, mental, and emotional healing. Can be done in person or long distance.

Nutrition

    Uses: All layers of healing. Especially beneficial for physical and emotional healing. Requires the recipient to ingest the nutrients. Can be done in person or long distance.

Past-Life

> Uses: All layers of healing. Especially beneficial for emotional and behavioral healing. Requires the recipient's active participation. Can be done in person or long distance.

Readings

> Uses: All layers of healing. Can be done in person or long distance.

Ritual Action

> Uses: All layers of healing. Best done in person, can be done long distance. Requires the recipient's active participation.

Soul Retrieval

> Uses: All layers of healing. Especially beneficial for healing the spiritual, mental, and emotional impacts of trauma. Can be done in person or long distance. Requires the recipient's active participation.

Sound

> Uses: All layers of healing. Especially beneficial for spiritual, emotional, and mental healing. Can be beneficial for any type of being and all species. Can be done in person or long distance.

Spirit Communication

> Uses: All layers of healing. For people in physical bodies this is especially beneficial for emotional healing. Can be done in person or long distance.

Stones, Crystals, & Minerals

> Uses: All layers of healing. Especially beneficial for emotional, spiritual, and mental healing. Can be beneficial for animals – either the animal alone or the animal and its people together. Can be done in person or long distance. Most effective when the recipient is physically near the stones or touching them. For long distance, give the recipient instructions about which stones to use and how to use them.

Yoga

> Uses: All layers of healing. Especially beneficial for physical and emotional healing. Must be done by the recipient.

APPENDIX B
GROUP LEARNING WITH THIS BOOK

It can be easier to learn healing techniques and concepts and to build your confidence when you share the journey with others. If you're so inclined, I encourage you to gather some like-minded friends or soon-to-be friends and share your healing skills, thoughts, philosophies, and questions. Here are some fun ways for healers to grow together:

♥ Each of you read segments of this book on your own and then discuss them within the group. Explore things like how you feel about what you read, what questions it brought up for you, what it inspired in you, how it challenged you…

♥ As a group discuss the things that inspire each of you about being a healer. Explore things like what draws you to this work, your visions about where you can go with this, your hopes for how your work will help others, your hopes for how your work will help you…

♥ As a group, discuss each of your concerns about being a healer. Explore things like your fears about doing this work, the types of situations you don't want to work with, the things you're uncertain of or insecure about, how you'll know if your work is effective…

♥ If you gather in-person, choose one healing technique or skill building tool per gathering and play with it together. Sometimes play lay all together, other times pair up or play in sub-groups. Make time for each of you to give and to receive.

   If your whole group can't gather in person, pair up and for the things that can be done long distance. For the ones that have to be done in person, play with someone local who may or may not be part of the group.

   After all of that beautiful learning and sharing, have a group discussion about your experiences of both giving and receiving. Include some honest feedback and plenty of loving encouragement.

♥ It can be really nice to end this type of gathering with a shared meal. This gives you each a bit more time to ground before returning to your other activities and more time to soak up the loving energy you've all just shared.

ABOUT THE AUTHOR

I'm a healer, shaman, and wisdom teacher; this is who I am everywhere I go and in everything I do. I love living on this foundation of spiritual depth and breadth combined with practical wisdom! The awareness I've grown into because of my work has opened my whole life to exciting experiences I never even thought about in earlier years. Was I born with special gifts? No. I was born curious and hungry.

In my first few years of learning to be a healer I gradually remembered how to experience life from outside of right and wrong, possible and impossible. I remembered the breadth of spiritual connection and innate wisdom that's readily available to all of us. I was on my way home to the person I knew how to be.

When I left my conventional job and began working as a healer, I had no idea what to call the path I was beginning to walk or all that would come into my life as a result. I just knew I was alive in a way I hadn't felt since early childhood. I felt a way of being human that echoed deep within my body and soul.

In the years since then I've enjoyed many teachers. Among them are people, life experience, the Earth, animals, plants, and souls beyond the physical world. I've gathered techniques and ideas by attending classes and workshops, reading, receiving and providing healing sessions, and observing life all around me.

Still now, after working with several thousand people from all over the world, each "ah-ha" moment I have personally and each one I witness someone else have, continues to inspire me to keep learning and stretching my awareness of how much wholeness we humans can actually live.

Looking back on my journey to where I am now, I know I've led myself along the perfect path for me for this lifetime. I live the magic every day. I know the continuity and connectivity of life beyond all doubt. I choose to be fully aware of the mixture of harmonies and disharmonies within me and in the world outside of me. I know how to help facilitate constructive wholeness on all levels of being and all planes of existence and I contribute something to that daily. The result for me is that I live the sparkle that delights every aspect of my soul.

I'm delighted that I gave my imagination permission to explore things that continually inspire me and my heart remembered how to sing!

Let your imagination explore things that continually inspire you.

INDEX OF TECHNIQUES & TOOLS